Castillo de San Marcos

A Guide to Castillo de San Marcos
National Monument
Florida

Produced by the
Division of Publications
National Park Service

U.S. Department of the Interior
Washington, D.C.

S. AVGVSTINI
pars est terra Florida
sub latitudine 30 grad.
ora vero maritima
humilior est, lan-
cinata et insu-
losa

Florida and the Pirates

This map, one of the earliest maps of a city that is now in the United States, depicts the June 1586 attack on St. Augustine by Sir Francis Drake. Note, in the middle, the English troops on Anastasia Island firing across the water on the Spanish fort.

Pages 2-3: *From the air the rationale for the layout of Castillo de San Marcos is readily apparent: no wall or approach is unguarded.*

On May 28, 1668, a ship anchored off St. Augustine harbor. It was a vessel from Veracruz, bringing flour from México. In the town, the drum sounded the alert for the garrison of 120 men. A launch went out to identify the newcomer and put the harbor pilot aboard. As it neared the ship, the crew on the launch hailed the Spaniards lining her gunwale. To the routine questions came the usual answers: Friends from México—come aboard! Two shots from the launch told the town the ship had been identified as friendly, and the seamen warped the launch alongside the ship. In St. Augustine, the people heard the signal shots and rejoiced. The soldiers returned their arms to the main guardhouse on the town plaza. Tomorrow the supplies would come ashore.

Unknown to the townspeople, when the launch pilot stepped aboard the supply ship, an alien crew of pirates swarmed out of hiding and leveled their guns at him and the others. He could do nothing but surrender.

Some time after midnight, a corporal was out on the bay fishing when he heard the sound of many oars pulling across the water. Something was not right. Desperately he paddled his little craft toward shore. The pirates, four boatloads of them, were right behind. Twice their shots found their mark, but he got to the fort where his shouts aroused the guards.

At the main guardhouse, a quarter mile from the fort, the sentries heard the shouting and the gunfire, but before they could respond, the pirates were upon them, a hundred strong. Out-numbered, the guards ran for the fort. Gov. Francisco de la Guerra rushed out of his house and, with the pirates pounding at his heels, joined the race for the fort. Somehow the garrison was able to beat back several assaults. In the confusion of darkness, however, the pirates seemed to be everywhere. They destroyed the weapons they found in the guardhouse and went on to the government house. Shouting and cursing, they scattered through the narrow streets, seizing or shooting the frightened, bewildered inhabitants.

Sgt. Maj. Nicolás Ponce de Léon, the officer responsible for defending the town, was at home, a sick man, covered with a greasy mercury salve and weak from the "sweatings" prescribed for his illness. On hearing the din, he roused himself and rushed to the guardhouse, only to find the pirates had been there first. He turned to the urgent task of shepherding his 70 unarmed soldiers and the others—men, women, and children—into the woods, leaving the pirates in complete possession of the town.

By daybreak the little force at the fort had lost five men, but they believed they had killed 11 pirates and wounded 19 others. Ponce came from the woods and reinforced the fort with his weaponless men. With daylight, two other vessels joined the ship from Veracruz. One was St. Augustine's own frigate, taken by the raiders near Havana, in which the pirates had been able to move in Spanish waters without detection. The other was the pirates' own craft. All three sailed into the bay, passed the cannon fire of the fort, anchored just out of range, and landed their remaining forces. Systematically they began to sack the town; no structure was neglected.

That afternoon, the governor sent out a sortie from the fort, but the leaders were wounded and the party retired. After 20 hours ashore, however, the pirates were ready to leave anyway, taking their booty, which probably amounted to only a few thousand pesos, and about 70 prisoners whom they had seized during the previous night's rampage. Just before leaving they ransomed most of their prisoners for meat, water, and firewood. The local Indians, however, they kept, claiming that the governor of Jamaica had told them to keep all Indians, blacks, and mulattoes as slaves, even if they were Spanish freemen. Finally on June 5 the raiders headed out to sea, amused as once again they passed the thunder of the useless guns in the old wooden fort as the small community grieved over its 60 dead and gave thanks for the ransomed prisoners.

The released prisoners identified the invaders as English and told how the enemy had carefully sounded the inlet, taken its latitude, and noted the landmarks. They intended to come back and seize the fort and make it a base for future operations against Spanish shipping.

To the Spaniards the attack on St. Augustine was far more than a pirate raid. St. Augustine, though isolated and small, was the keystone in the defense of Florida, a way station on Spain's great commercial route. Each year, galleons bearing the proud Iberian banners sailed past the coral keys and surf-pounded beaches of Florida, following the Gulf Stream on the way to Cádiz. Each galleon carried a treasure of gold and silver from the mines of Perú and México—and all Europe knew it.

A shipload of treasure, dispatched from México by Hernán Cortés in 1522, never reached the Spanish court. A French corsair attacked the Spanish ship and the treasure ended up in Paris, not Madrid. Soon, daring adventurers of all nationalities sailed for the West Indies and Spanish treasure. Florida's position on the lifeline connecting Spain with her colonies gave this sandy peninsula strategic importance. Spain knew that Florida must be defended to prevent enemies from using the harbors for preying upon Spanish commerce and to give safe haven to shipwrecked Spanish mariners.

The French, ironically, brought the situation to a head in 1564 when they established Fort Caroline, a colony named for their teenage king, Charles IX, near the mouth of Florida's St. Johns River. A year later Spanish Admiral Pedro Menéndez de Avilés came to Florida, established the St. Augustine colony, and forthwith removed the Frenchmen, suspected of piracy. This small fortified settlement on Florida's northeast coast and Havana in Cuba anchored opposite ends of the passage through the Straits of Florida enabling Spanish ships to pass safely from the Gulf of Mexico out into the Atlantic.

A typical early fort was San Juan de Pinos, burned by English sailor Francis Drake in 1586. Drake took the fort's bronze artillery and a considerable amount of money. San Juan consisted of a pine stockade around small buildings for gunpowder storage and quarters. Cannon were mounted atop a broad platform, or cavalier, so they could fire over the stockade. Such forts could be built quickly, but they could also be destroyed easily. If Indian fire arrows, enemy attack, or mutinies failed, then hurricanes, time, and

Sir Francis Drake's attack on St. Augustine was part of the growing hostilities between Spain and England that culminated in the attack of the Spanish Armada on England two years later. Drake was also the first sea captain to take his own ship all the way around the world. Ferdinand Magellan's ship had made the trip 57 years earlier, but Magellan had been killed in the Philippines.

Spain in the Caribbean, 1717-1748

Spain, England, and France vied for the land and wealth of the New World. This map, while not showing actual settlement and possession of the land shows what each nation thought was theirs. Spain's dominions were more extensive than those of Britain or France, for the Spaniards were the first to explore and to begin to claim and settle the land.

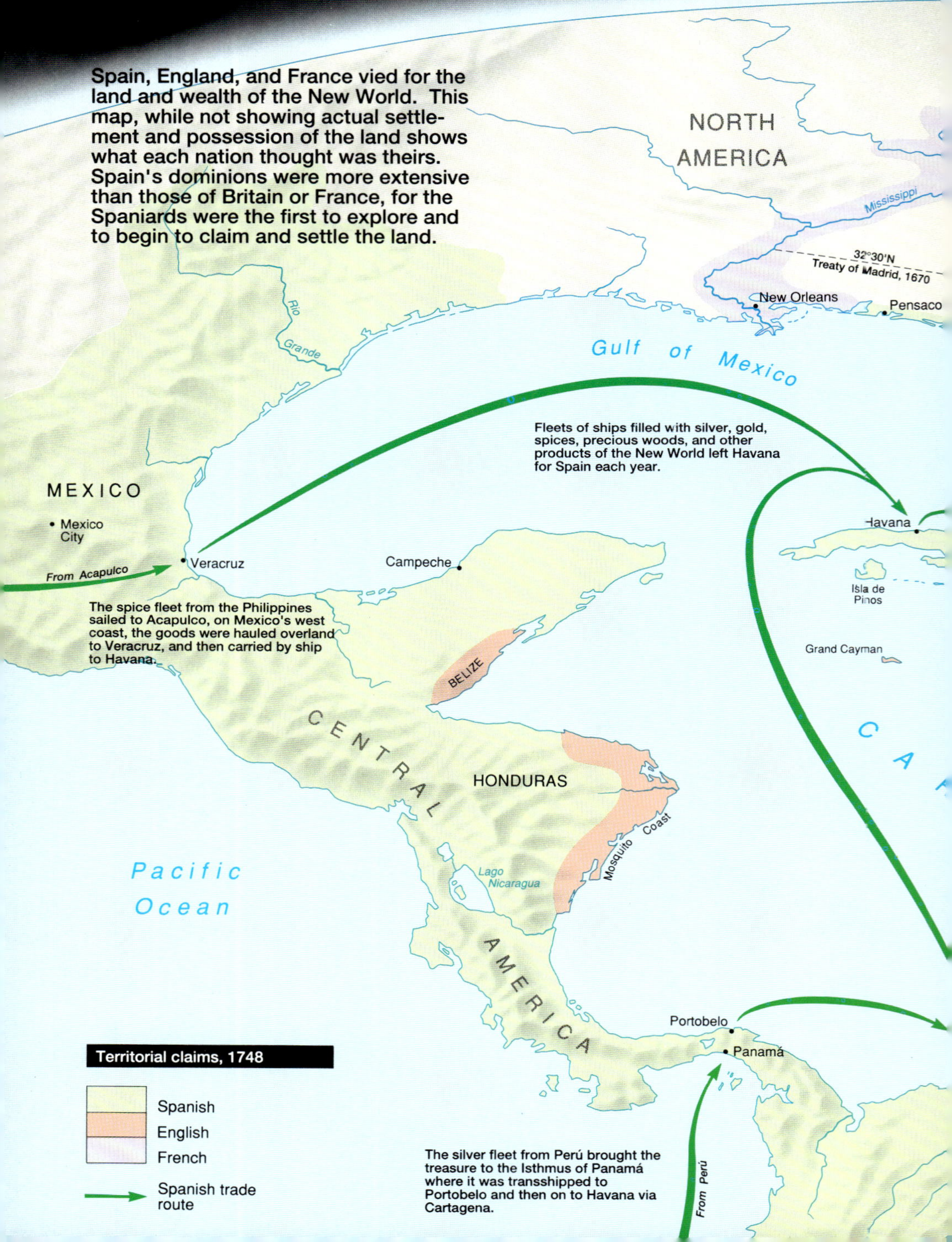
NORTH AMERICA
Mississippi
32°30'N
Treaty of Madrid, 1670
New Orleans
Pensaco
Rio Grande
Gulf of Mexico
Fleets of ships filled with silver, gold, spices, precious woods, and other products of the New World left Havana for Spain each year.
MEXICO
Mexico City
Veracruz
From Acapulco
Campeche
Havana
Isla de Pinos
Grand Cayman
The spice fleet from the Philippines sailed to Acapulco, on Mexico's west coast, the goods were hauled overland to Veracruz, and then carried by ship to Havana.
BELIZE
CENTRAL AMERICA
HONDURAS
Mosquito Coast
Lago Nicaragua
Pacific Ocean
Portobelo
Panamá
Territorial claims, 1748
Spanish
English
French
Spanish trade route
The silver fleet from Perú brought the treasure to the Isthmus of Panamá where it was transshipped to Portobelo and then on to Havana via Cartagena.
From Perú

Ohio
James
Jamestown
New York
NEW ENGLAND
CAROLINA
Port Royal
Charleston
Roanoke Island
GEORGIA
Savannah
Apalache Fort
St. Augustine
To Spain via Gulf Stream
FLORIDA
Florida Keys
Straits of Florida
Nassau
Eleuthera
BAHAMAS
CUBA
Santiago de Cuba
GREATER ANTILLES
JAMAICA
Kingston
HISPANIOLA
HAITI
SANTO DOMINGO
Santo Domingo
Atlantic Ocean
PUERTO RICO
San Juan
Virgin Islands
LESSER ANTILLES
CARIBBEAN SEA
Cartagena
Aruba
Curacao
LESSER ANTILLES
Lago de Maracaibo
Magdalena
SOUTH AMERICA
VENEZUELA
Margarita
Spanish St. Augustine served as the northernmost outpost of the Caribbean, watching over the waters of the Gulf stream, Spain's highway to Europe.

Pedro Menéndez de Avilés (1519-74) was the founder of St. Augustine and first governor of Florida. He struggled throughout his life to put St. Augustine on a firm footing, fending off French efforts to destroy his settlement. The engraving is a copy of a portrait by Titian that was destroyed in a fire at the end of the last century.

termites were certain to do the job. During the first 100 years of Spanish settlement, nine wooden forts one after another were built at St. Augustine.

Spain did not yet see the need for an impregnable fort here. After the English failures at Roanoke Island in North Carolina in 1586-87, the weak settlement of Jamestown, Virginia, a few years later did not impress the powerful Council of the Indies in Madrid as a threat to Spanish interests. Moreover, the Franciscans, by extending the mission frontier deep into Indian lands, put the Spanish stamp of occupation upon a vast territory. The fallacy in this thinking lay in underestimating the colonizing ability of the English and believing that an Indian friendly to Spain would never become a friend of England.

The defeat of the powerful Spanish Armada in 1588 was a dramatic harbinger of things to come; the way was clear for England to extend its control of the seas. Its great trading companies were active on the coasts of four continents, and powerful English nobles strove for possessions beyond the seas. Jamestown, despite its inauspicious beginning, was soon followed by the settlements in New England and elsewhere. Between the James River and Spanish Florida stretched a vast, rich territory too tempting to ignore, and in 1665 Charles II of England granted a patent for its occupation. The boundaries of the new colony of Carolina brazenly included some hundred miles or more of Spanish-occupied land— even St. Augustine itself!

The signs were clear: The fight for Florida was inevitable.

In the middle 1600s at St. Augustine, just south of where the Castillo now stands, there was a wooden fort. It was almost as large as the Castillo, but it was a fort only in name. Most of the timbers were rotten. Smallpox had killed so many Indians that there were not enough laborers to carry in replacement logs.

Money to maintain the outposts came from New Spain, for, the government in Madrid reasoned, the Florida forts protected the commercial routes from México to Spain. Consequently, officials in México City had to find the silver to pay the troops and buy the food, clothing, and other supplies that Florida so desperately needed. Despite the orders from Madrid, payments from México City were always behind, as Floridians knew from bitter experience.

Yet, if ever there was a time to protect Spanish interests in Florida, it was now. The English had attacked Santo Domingo and captured Jamaica. The Dutch had been seen in Apalache Bay on Florida's west coast. As the corsairs grew bolder, one governor made this appraisal: "In spite of the great valor with which we would resist, successful defense would be doubtful" without stronger defenses.

Proposals for a permanent, stone fort dated back to 1586 after the discovery of the native shellstone, coquina. For years officials in Spain, México, and Florida argued about what needed to be done. By 1668 payments and sufficient supplies of food were eight years behind. The townspeople and the soldiers lived in poverty and the old wooden fort was on the verge of falling into the sea.

The sack of St. Augustine was a blessing in disguise, for it shocked Spanish officials into action. The governor of Havana lent 1,200 pesos for masting and rigging St. Augustine's frigate, thus ensuring the presidio's communication with its supply bases. The viceroy released the 1669 payroll plus money for general repairs, weapons, gunpowder, and lead for bullets. He also promised 75 men to bring the troop levels to authorized strength. And St. Augustine was allowed to keep an 18-pounder bronze cannon that had been salvaged from a shipwreck. This aid—12 months of life for the colony—totaled at least 110,000 pesos. Included was the hire of mules for the 75 recruits to ride from México City to Veracruz. Hiring the animals was easier than finding men, however. Fifty-one of them arrived at last in 1670; the rest had deserted or died. Officials in St. Augustine, however, were not sure that the new troops were particularly loyal to Spanish interests.

It was Mariana, Queen Regent of Spain, who gave permanent aid to St. Augustine in three decrees addressed to the viceroy. On March 11, 1669, she ordered him to pay the Florida funds on time and add a proper amount for building the fortification proposed by the governor. Next, on April 10, she commanded him to support a full 300-man garrison in Florida instead of the customary 257 soldiers and 43 missionaries. Finally, on October 30, she enjoined him to consult with the governor about an adequate fortification and provide for its construction.

Beginning the Castillo

To show her commitment to the proposed construction, the Queen Regent appointed Sgt. Maj. Don Manuel de Cendoya, a veteran of 22 years service, as successor to Governor Guerra.

In México City Cendoya followed Queen Mariana's orders and delivered his message to the viceroy, the Marquis de Mancera. Florida's defenses were to be strengthened at once with a main castillo at St. Augustine, a second fort to protect the harbor entrance, and a third to prevent troop landings. Initial estimates were that the project would cost 30,000 pesos. At this point came the news of the English settlement at Charleston, and Cendoya at once suggested a fourth fort at Santa Catalina.

The viceroy's finance council finally decided to allot 12,000 pesos to begin work on one fort. If suitable progress were made, they would consider sending 10,000 yearly until completion. The question of additional forts would be referred to the crown. Cendoya had to be satisfied with this arrangement and a levy of 17 soldiers. He left for Florida, making a stop at Havana where he sought skilled workers. There he also found an engineer, Ignacio Daza.

On August 8, 1671, a month after Cendoya's arrival in St. Augustine, the first worker began to draw pay. By the time the mosquitoes were sluggish in the cooler fall weather, the quarrymen had opened coquina pits on Anastasia Island, and the lime burners were building two big kilns just north of the old fort. The carpenters put up a palm-thatched shelter at the quarry, built a dozen rafts for ferrying stone, firewood, and oyster shells for the limekilns across the water. They built boxes, handbarrows, and carretas—the long, narrow, hauling wagons—as well. The blacksmith hammered out axes, picks, stonecutters' hatchets, crowbars, shovels, spades, hoes, wedges, and nails for the carpenters. The grindstone screeched as the cutting edge went on the tools.

Indians at the quarry chopped out the dense

Stone masons were the most skilled and highly paid laborers who worked on the Castillo.

thickets of scrub oak and palmetto, driving out the rattlesnakes and clearing the ground for the shovelmen to uncover the top layer of coquina. Day after day Diego Díaz Mejía, the overseer, kept the picks and axes going, cutting deep groves into the soft yellow stone, while with wedge and bar the workers broke loose and pried up the blocks—small pieces that a single man could shoulder, and tremendously heavy cubes two feet thick and twice as long that six strong men could hardly lift.

Díaz watched his workers heave the finest stone on the wagons. He sent the oxen plodding to the wharf at the head of a marshy creek, where the load of rough stone was carefully balanced on the rafts for ferrying to the building site. And on the opposite shore of the bay, next to the old fort, the cache of unhewn stone grew larger daily, and the stonecutters shaped the soft coquina for the masons.

In the limekilns, oyster shells glowed white-hot and changed into fine quality, quicksetting lime. By spring of 1672, there were 4,000 *fanegas* (about 7,000 bushels) of lime in the two storehouses and great quantities of hewn and rough stone.

Although the real construction had not even started, great obstacles had already been overcome. Maintaining an adequate work force and skilled workers was a continual problem. When there should have been 150 men to keep the 15 artisans working at top speed—50 in the quarries and hauling stone, 50 for gathering oyster shells and helping at the kilns, and another 50 for digging foundation trenches, toting the excavation baskets, and mixing mortar—it was hard to get as many as 100 laborers on the job.

Indians from three nations, the Guale (coastal Georgia), Timucua (Florida east of the Aucilla River), and Apalache (between the Aucilla and the Apalachicola), were employed. True, they were paid labor, but some had to travel more than 200 miles to reach the presidio, and many served unwillingly. In theory each complement of Indian labor served only a certain length of time; in practice it was not uncommon for the men to be held long past their assigned time, either through necessity or carelessness.

Indians were used as unskilled laborers and paid the lowest wages—one *real* (about 20 cents) per day plus corn rations. Most labored at the monotonous, back-straining work in the quarries. A few were trained as carpenters and received correspondingly greater wages but never the equal of what the Europeans earned. One Indian was trained as a stonecutter and worked on the Castillo for 16 years.

Besides Indian labor, there were a few Spanish workers paid 4 *reales* per day, and a number of convicts, either local or from Caribbean ports. Beginning in 1679 there were seven blacks and mulattoes among the convicts. Eighteen black slaves belonging to the crown joined the labor gang in 1687. Convicts and slaves received rations but no wage. A typical convict might have been a Spaniard caught smuggling English goods into the colony, who was condemned to six years' labor on the fortifications. If he tried to escape, the term was doubled and he faced the grim prospect of being sent to a fever-infested African presidio to work.

The military engineer, Ignacio Daza, was paid the top wage of 3 pesos (about $4.75) per day. Daza died seven months after coming to Florida, so the crown paid only the surprisingly small sum of 546 pesos (about $862) for engineering services in starting the greatest of Spanish Florida fortifications.

Of the artisans, there were Lorenzo Lajones, master of construction, and two master masons, each of whom received the master workman's wage of 20 *reales* (about $4). Seven masons and eight stonecutters at 12 *reales*, and 12 carpenters whose pay ranged from 6 to 12 *reales*, completed the ranks of the skilled workers. Later, some of these wages were reduced: Lajones' successor as master of construction was paid only 17 *reales*, the master mason 13, and the stonecutters from 3 to 11 *reales*, with half of them at the 3- and 4-*real* level.

These were few men for the job at hand, and to speed the work along Governor Cendoya used any prisoner including neighboring Carolinians who fell into Spanish hands. In 1670, a vessel bound for Charleston, mistakenly put in at Santa Catalina Mission, the Spanish post near the Savannah River, and William Carr and John Rivers were taken. A rescue sloop sent from Charleston protested the Spaniards' actions, with Joseph Bailey and John Collins carrying the message from the English. For their trouble, they were dispatched with Rivers and Carr to St. Augustine to labor on the fort.

Three of the prisoners were masons, and their

Great numbers of local Indians carried out the many heavy-duty tasks that kept this labor-intensive project continually moving forward.

Spanish silver coins were used throughout the Caribbean and the British colonies. Often they were cut in two, or quartered, or even cut into eight pieces, giving rise to our expression, "two bits, four bits, six bits, a dollar," bit meaning the number of pieces of one coin needed to make a dollar. The coins shown here are a 2-real, a 1-real, and another 2-real piece. On the one 2-real coin, note the Chinese characters indicating that the coin had been used in trade in the Orient. The profile is that of Charles III, who had died in 1788, though the inscription says that it is of Charles IV. The diemaker simply changed the date and added another "I" rather than using the more conventional "IV" roman numeral designation for 4.

Spanish names—Bernardo Patricio (for Bernard Fitzpatrick), and Juan Calens (for John Collins), and Guillermo Car (for William Carr)—were duly written on the payrolls. Some of these British subjects became permanent residents. Carr, for instance, embraced first the Catholic faith and then Juana de Contreras, by whom he fathered eight children. His father-in-law was a corporal, a circumstance that may have helped Carr enlist as a gunner while also working as a highly paid stonecutter.

The Spaniards were understandably cautious in relying on the loyalty of foreigners, but actually the new subjects served well. John Collins especially pleased the officials. He could burn more lime in a week than others could in twice the time. And as a prisoner he had to be paid only 8 *reales* instead of the 20 due a master workman. Like Carr, Collins seemed to like St. Augustine. He rose steadily in the crown's employ from master of the kilns to quarrymaster, with dugouts, provisions, and convicts all in his charge. When pirates landed on Anastasia in 1683 and marched on the city, Carr made sure that all crown property in the quarry was moved to safety. Royal recognition honored his loyalty and years of service.

A few years later 11 Englishmen were captured several miles north of St. Augustine. All were committed to the labor gang—except Andrew Ransom. He was to be garroted. On the appointed day Ransom ascended the scaffold. The executioner put the rope collar about his neck. The screw was turned 6 times—and the rope broke! Ransom breathed again.

While the onlookers marveled, the friars took the incident as an act of God and led Ransom to sanctuary in the parish church. Word reached the governor that this man was an ingenious fellow, an artillerist, a carpenter, and what was most remarkable, a maker of "artificial fires"—fire bombs. Ransom was offered his life if he would put his talents to use at the Castillo. He agreed and, like Collins, was exceedingly helpful. Twelve years later, church authorities finally agreed that the sanctuary granted by the parish pastor was valid. At last Ransom was free of the garrote.

All told, between 100 and 150 workers on the construction crew labored in those first days of feverish preparations. They, along with some 500 others—

including about 100 soldiers in the garrison, a few
Franciscan friars, a dozen mariners, and the townspeople—had to be fed. When supplies from México
did not come, getting food was even harder than
finding workers, especially since the coastal soil at
St. Augustine yielded poorly to 17th-century agri-
cultural methods.

Of the crops grown at St. Augustine, Indian corn
was the staple. Most of the planting, cultivating, and
harvesting of extensive fields near the town was done
by Indians. At times as many as 300 Indians, including those working on the fortification, served the
crown at the presidio. To make the food, whether
grown locally or shipped in from México, go as far as
possible, it was rationed: 3 pounds daily until 1679,
then 2½ pounds until 1684, then 2 pounds until 1687,
and finally 2½ again. Convicts also got corn if flour
was not on hand, and they also received a meat
ration. Fresh meat was rather scarce, but the waters
teemed with fish and shellfish. A paid fisherman kept
the men supplied.

Garden vegetables were few. Squash grew well in
the sandy soil, as did beans and sweet potatoes,
citron, pomegranates, figs, and oranges. And of
course there were onions and garlic. But St. Augustine was never self-supporting. After a century of
existence, it still depended for its very life upon
supplies from México.

As the long, hot days of the second summer
shortened into fall, Governor Cendoya saw that after
a year of gathering men and materials, he was ready
to start building.

Daza and the governor decided to construct the
Castillo on the west shore of the bay just north of
the old fort. It was a site that would take advantage
of every natural feature for the best possible defensive position. The new fort, they decided, would be
similar, though somewhat larger. In line with the
more recent ideas, Daza recommended a slight
lengthening of the bastions. All around the castillo
they planned a broad, deep moat and beyond the
moat, a high palisade on the three land sides.

It was a simple and unpretentious plan, but a good
one. Daza, schooled in the Italian-Spanish principles
of fortification that grew out of the 16th-century
designs of Franceso de Marchi, was clearly a practi-
cal man. His plan called for a "regular" fort—that is,

Yo Juan moreno y segobia scriuano pu.co de
propiedad desta ciudad y Precidio de san aug.n de
la florida doy fee y verdadero testimonio a los q. esta
los señores que el presente vieren como oy domingo a
cosa de las q.tro de la tarde que se quentan dos dias del
presente mes de octubre de mill y seiscientos y setenta y dos
años estando junto a la fuerça deste precidio donde esta
señalada la planta de la nueba fuerça que por horden
de su magestad se a de fabricar de piedra el señor su per-
tor mayor don manuel de sendoça gouernador y capitan
jeneral destas Prouincias Por su magestad en su Real
nombre acompañado con los Jueces officiales Reales su
Pherador mayor don nicolas Ponçe de leon y capitan antonio
de arguelles que lo son Por su magestad deste precidio y otras
muchas personas y reformados del, con una açada en
las manos y los demas circunstantes y oficiales me-
tieron principio este dho dia a abrir los cimientos para comenzar la fabrica del dho castillo como de fueron
jurando este dho dia y yo el escriuano fui presente y
para que dello conste de mandamiento del señor gouernador y capitan jeneral doy el presente en la ciudad
de san augustin de la florida en el dho dia siendo tes-
tigos el capitan antonio de arguelles que lo es y otros tes-
tigos Por su magestad los capitanes lorenso joseph de leon
Juan enrique de rribera Vecinos y reformados en este
precidio, y ba escrito en papel comun Por quanto en este
precidio no corre el sellado de que doy fee =

Comissiono ✠ En testim.º de verdad

Juan moreno y segobia
s.no pu.co

a symmetrical structure. Basically it was a square with a bastion at each corner. Equally strong on all sides, this design was ideal for Florida's low, flat terrain.

About four o'clock Sunday afternoon, October 2, 1672, Governor Cendoya walked to a likely looking spot between the strings marking out the lines of the new fortification and thrust a spade into the earth, as Juan Moreno y Segovia, reported the ground breaking ceremonies for Queen Mariana.

Little more than a month later on Wednesday, November 9, Cendoya laid the first stone of the foundation. The people of St. Augustine must have wept for joy. All were glad and proud, the aged soldiers who had given a lifetime of service to the crown, the four orphans whose father had died in the pirate raid a few years earlier, the widows and their children, the craftsmen, the workers, and the royal officials. But none could have been more pleased or proud than Don Manuel de Cendoya. He of all the Florida governors had the honor to begin the first permanent Florida fortification.

Laying the foundations was not easy, for the soil was sandy and low and as winter came the Indians were struck by *El Contagio*—a smallpox epidemic. The laboring force dwindled to nothing. The governor asked the crown to have Havana send 30 slaves. Meanwhile, Cendoya himself and his soldiers took to the shovels. As they dug a trench some 17 feet wide and 5 feet deep, the masons came in and laid two courses of heavy stones directly on the hard-packed sand bottom for the foundation. The work was slow, for high tide flooded the trenches.

About 1½ feet inside the toe of this broad 2-foot-high foundation, the masons stretched a line marking the scarp or curtain, a wall that would gradually taper upward from a 13-foot base to about 9 feet at its top, 20 feet above the foundation. In the 12 months that followed, the north, south, and east walls rose steadily. By midsummer of 1673 the east side was 12 feet high, and the presidio was jubilant over the news that the viceroy was sending even more money.

This good news was tempered by the viceroy's assertion that he would release no more money for the work without a direct order from the crown. Cendoya had already asked the queen to raise the allowance to 16,000 pesos a year so the construction could be finished in four years. For, as he put it, the English menace at Charleston brooked no delay. The English were said to be outfitting ships for an invasion.

Gradually, however, construction slowed. In 1673 Cendoya and Daza died within a few days of one another. The governor's mantle fell upon Major Ponce, in whom the local Spaniards had little confidence.

Trouble beset Ponce on every side. The viceroy was reluctant to part with money for this project despite evidence that English strength and influence was increasing daily, especially among the Indians. Shortly after Ponce took control, a terrific storm hit the city. High tides undermined houses, flooded fields and gardens, and polluted the wells. Sickness took its toll. The old wooden fort was totally ruined. Waves washed out a bastion, causing it to collapse under the weight of its guns. The other seaward bastion and the palisade were also breached in several places.

Then in the spring of 1675 when another provision ship was lost, Ponce had to lead a group of workers on a long march into Timucua to fetch provisions from the Indians. Only a few masons were left to carry on the work at the Castillo.

Despite all these problems, Ponce made progress. The north curtain was completed and the east and south were well underway. But looking west the soldiers could see only open country.

On May 3, 1675, the long-awaited supply ship from México safely arrived. Among its few passengers was a new governor for Florida, Sgt. Maj. Don Pablo de Hita Salazar, a hard-bitten veteran of campaigns in Europe, and most recently governor of Veracruz. Surely it was because of his reputation as a soldier that he was assigned to Florida. Besides continuing the work on the fort he was ordered to "dislocate" the Charleston settlement. Led to believe the viceroy would help in the difficult task ahead, Hita, in fact, found that official singularly reluctant.

At St. Augustine, the work had been dragging, but Hita made some positive points in writing the crown: "Although I have seen many castillos of consequence and reputation in the form of its plan, this one is not surpassed by any of those of greater character." Furthermore, he endorsed the statement of the royal officials, who were eager to point out the brighter side of the picture: "If it had to be built in another place than St. Augustine it would cost a double amount because there will not be the advantage of having the laborers, at a *real* of wages each day, with such meagre sustenance as three pounds of maize, nor will the overseers and artisans work in other places with such little salaries . . . nor will the stone, lime, and other materials be found so close at hand and with the convenience there is in this presidio."

So much money—34,298 pesos—had been spent on the fort, and it was not yet finished, so it was important to tell the authorities the positive benefits of this project, for at this point the old stockade was a ruin and the new one was unusable. Reports from English deserters told them that Charleston, less than 215 miles to the north, was well defended by a stockade and 20 cannon.

Using characteristic realism, energy, and enthusiasm that would have done credit to a much younger man, Don Pablo set about making his own fortification defensible. The bastion of San Carlos—at the northeast corner of the Castillo—was the nearest to completion. Hita ordered it finished so that cannon could be mounted on its rampart.

While the masons were busy at that work, he took his soldiers and razed the old fort. The best of its wood went into a barrier across the open west side of the Castillo. In 15 days they built a 12-foot-high earthwork with two half-bastions, faced with a veneer of stone and fronted by a moat 14 feet wide and 10 feet deep. At last the garrison had four walls for protection.

Next the powder magazine in the gorge of San Carlos was completed and a ramp laid over it to give access to the rampart above. The three curtains rose to their full height of 20 feet. At the southeast corner the workers dumped hundreds of baskets of sand and rubble into the void formed by the walls of San Agustin bastion and filled it to the 20-foot level.

Both carpenters and masons worked on the temporary buildings and finished a little powder magazine near the north curtain. A timber-framed coquina structure, partitioned into guardhouse, lieutenant's quarters, armory, and provision magazine, took shape along the west wall. Finally, a few of the guns from the old fort were mounted in San Carlos and San Agustín bastions and along the west front. After three years of work, the Castillo was a defense at last.

Archeology, in one of its functions, provides us with glimpses into the life of days gone by. The three bone buttons were found in and around the Castillo. The light-colored, smooth button with one hole was found in a sentry box. Perhaps a coat caught on the entryway and the button tore off, never to be found by the owner? The brass button is from a 19th-century Spanish uniform.

And now Governor Hita's first admiration for its design vanished. The Castillo, he said, was too massive. Surely no one would ever besiege it formally. Rather, the danger lay in a blockade of the harbor or occupation of Anastasia Island, actions that would cut the presidio's lifeline. The San Carlos bastion was too high for effective fire on the inlet or to sweep Anastasia. He argued that the Castillo, including the parapet, should be held to a total height of only 20 feet and supplemented by a 6-gun redoubt directly facing the inlet.

Royal officials strenuously opposed the governor's attempts to change Daza's plan. They wrote the crown of Hita's desire to tear finished walls down to the level he thought proper.

In Hita's view the west wall, though temporary, was adequate. Therefore he would defer the permanent wall and start instead on the permanent guardroom, quarters, ravelin, and moat. Royal officials insisted, however, that since the west wall was nothing but a half-rotten fence and a mound of earth faced with stone, all the walls must be completed as soon as possible.

In the hope that the crown would agree to lower the walls, Hita let the work lag on the two seaward bastions while he began the west wall and bastions. Construction continued despite trouble with the Choctaws, despite the worrisome impossibility of driving out the Carolina settlers, despite the pirate raid on the port of Apalache in the west, and the ever-present fear of invasion. Lorenzo Lajones, the master of construction, died, but still the work went on. Even after the viceroy's 10,000 pesos were spent, work continued with money diverted from the troop payroll. As a last resort, people gave what they could out of their own poverty. When these gifts were gone, the scrape of the trowel ceased and the hammer and axe were laid aside. Construction stopped on the last day of 1677.

At the same time, the supply vessel bringing desperately needed provisions and clothing from México arrived, only to be lost on a sand bar right in St. Augustine harbor. It was a heartbreaking loss. Hita became disconsolate. The help he begged from Havana never came, and for four years his reports to the viceroy were ignored. Old, discouraged, and sick, Hita wrote the crown that he was "without human recourse" in this remote province. Perhaps the final blow to his pride was a terse order from the crown to stick strictly to Daza's plan for the Castillo.

Yet the old warrior did not give up. Eventually the viceroy released 5,000 more pesos, and after 20 months of idleness construction resumed on August 29, 1679. As soon as Hita left his sickbed he was back at the fort, impatient with the snail's pace of progress under a new master of construction, Juan Márquez Molina from Havana, whose sharp-eyed inspections found stones missing from their courses and some of the walls too thin.

The royal officials, always on hand to make sure the governor followed the crown's directives to the letter, blamed the deficiencies on Hita, "who has trod this fort down without knowledge of the art of fortification." With another 5,000 pesos plus the masons due to arrive from Havana, said the old man in rebuttal, "I promise to leave the work in very good condition." Before he could make good on that promise, Sgt. Maj. Don Juan Márquez Cabrera arrived at the end of November 1680 to take over the reins of government.

So, half apologizing for his own little knowledge of "architecture and geometry," Hita left the trials and tribulations of this frontier province to his more youthful successor.

Actually, Hita had done a great deal. Within six weeks after his arrival he had made the Castillo defensible against any but an overwhelming force. During the rest of his 5½-year term he brought the walls up to where they were ready for the parapet builders, despite one obstacle after another. In fact, the parapet on San Carlos bastion was almost complete, with embrasures for the artillery and firing steps for the musketeers. The only low part of the work was the San Pablo bastion, where the level had been miscalculated. The sally port had its drawbridge and iron-bound portal, and another heavy door closed the postern in the north curtain. Permanent rooms that would go along the curtain walls were still only plans, but in a temporary building centered in the courtyard were a guardroom and storeroom, and a little chapel stood near the postern in the shadow of the north curtain.

The new man, Major Juan Márquez Cabrera, formerly governor of Honduras, checked the Castillo

These bottles, dating from the 19th-century American presence in St. Augustine, attest to the continuity of life. The shells on the stoneware flask indicate that it has been in saltwater for some time. The gold and tan bottle originally held ginger beer, a popular drink in the mid-1800s. The green bottle is stamped "Rumford Chemical Works" of Rumford, Rhode Island, on the shoulder.

Although Saint Augustine was primarily a military outpost intended to protect Spain's dominion over Florida and the sea route of its treasure fleets, Saint Augustine also became a viable community as well, home to the settler-soldiers and their families. Except for the Castillo, which was finished in 1695, hardly any structure survives from Saint Augustine's first 150 years. Archeological investigations show that almost all the earliest dwellings were small, crude structures made of local materials with thatched roofs and bare, dirt floors; coquina, the stone used in building the fort was not used for homes until 1690. The ordinary wear and tear of weather and time ensured that none of these early structures lasted.

Archeology can tell us about the lives of the people who lived in these houses, for more than 1,000 objects and pieces and bits of pottery dating to the 16th century have been found. Most of them are from local Indian sources and corroborate written records that show that by 1600 almost 25 percent of the soldiers had taken Indian wives because few Spanish women initially came to Florida. Besides using their local ceramics, the Indian women introduced New World foods to their families and into the

The Oldest House Museum

View in St. George Street

Spanish diet, creating something that was neither wholly Spanish nor wholly Indian.

The town itself was laid out according to ordinances dictated by the Spanish government in 1563, resulting in a carefully planned community with houses fronting directly on standard-width streets with gardens in the rear or at the side. This showed clearly that Spain intended St. Augustine to be a permanent settlement, not a mere outpost on the fringes of empire. In the 18th century, indeed, it had become a vibrant community that numbered almost 3,000 persons when the garrison and all inhabitants withdrew after Florida became British in 1763.

The community and the people who lived in it were a mixture of influences showing graphically how quickly Spaniards adapted to the New World, using its materials, changing patterns that they had brought from their homeland to meet new conditions, and creating a society that simulated, but did not mirror, what they had left behind. Saint Augustine was the beginning of a new world for those who came here in 1565.

The map, based on the surveys of Juan de Solís, was drawn in 1764, a year after the British took control of Florida. English names have already been given to the town's features. Somehow Fort St. Mark, a translation of Castillo de San Marcos, does not have the same ring.

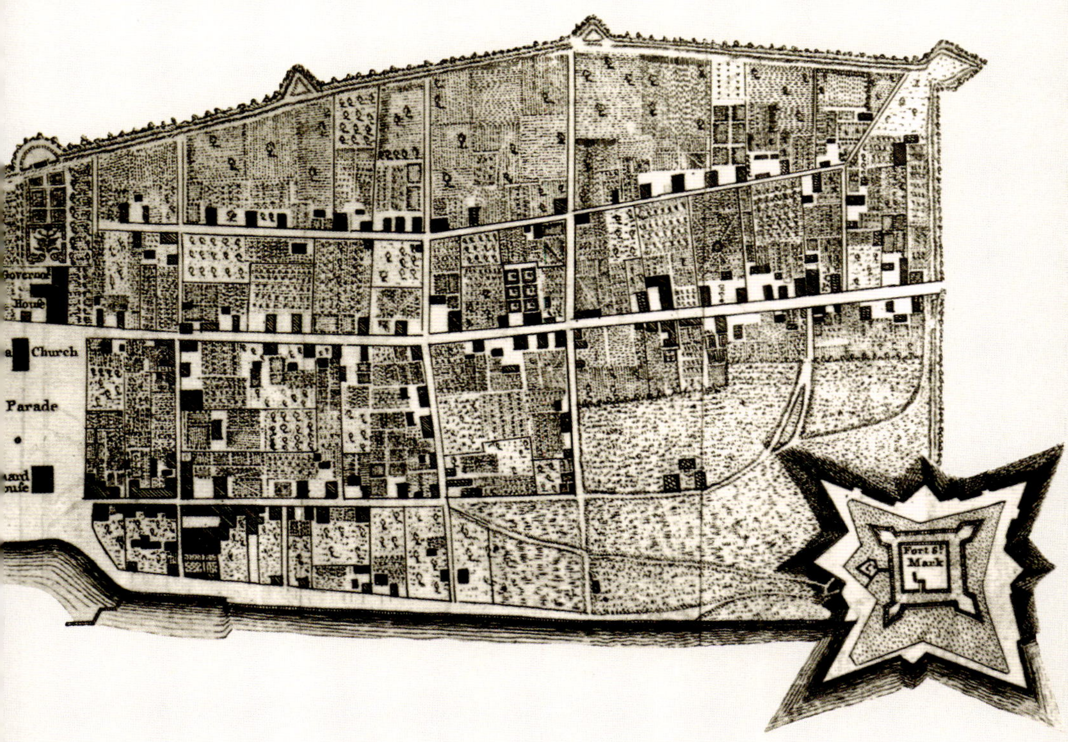

work carefully with the construction master. Those long years without an engineer had left them a heritage of mistakes—skimpy foundations, levels miscalculated—that had to be set right. From Havana came a military engineer, Ensign Don Juan de Císcara. During his brief stay he gave valuable guidance for continuing the work, built the ramp to San Pablo bastion, and laid foundations for the ravelin and its moat wall.

The 1680s were turbulent years. In 1682, the year the ravelin was finished, a dozen or so pirate craft in the Straits of Florida seized numerous Spanish prizes, including the Florida frigate on its way to Veracruz. They raided Mosquito Inlet, only 60 miles south of St. Augustine. In the west, pirates struck Fort San Marcos de Apalache and even went up the San Martín (Suwanee) River to rob cattle ranches in Timucua.

Work on the Castillo fell further and further behind schedule. Márquez appealed to the curate for dispensation to work on Sundays and holy days. Because of a history of bad relations with Márquez, the request was refused. Márquez appealed to higher authorities. When approval came, however, it was too late, for invasion came first.

On March 30, 1683, English corsairs landed a short way south of the *Centinela de Matanzas*, the watchtower, at Matanzas Inlet near the south end of Anastasia Island and about 14 miles from St. Augustine. Under cover of darkness, a few of the raiders came up behind the tower and surprised the sentries.

The march on St. Augustine began the next day. Fortunately a soldier from St. Augustine happened by Matanzas and saw the motley band. Posthaste he warned the governor, who sent Capt. Antonio de Argüelles with 30 musketeers to meet them on Anastasia. A mile from the presidio the pirates walked into the captain's ambush. After exchanging a few shots—one of which lodged in Argüelles' leg—the Englishmen beat a hasty retreat down the island to their boats. They sailed to St. Augustine and anchored at the inlet in plain sight of the unfinished Castillo.

Márquez, his soldiers, and the townspeople worked day and night to strengthen the Castillo. Missing parapets and a firing step were improvised from dry stone. Expecting the worst, everybody crowded into the fort. But the corsairs, looking at the stone fort and nursing their wounds, decided to sail on.

After this scare, the Castillo crew worked with renewed zeal. By mid-1683 they had completed the San Agustín and San Pablo bastions. Governor Márquez sent the crown a wooden model to show what had been done.

This was progress made in the face of privation— hunger that made the people demand of Márquez that he buy supplies from a stray Dutch trader from New York. It was unlawful, but the people had to eat. Imagine the joy in the presidio soon afterward when two subsidy payments came at one time! Márquez gave the soldiers two years' back pay and had enough provisions on hand for 14 months. The 27 guns of the presidio, from the iron 2-pounder to the 40-pounder bronze, all had their gunner's ladle, rammer, sponge, and wormer, along with plenty of powder and shot. There was also an alarm bell in San Carlos bastion.

By August 1684 Governor Márquez started on the fort rooms and finished them the next spring. Court-yard walls paralleled the four curtains, and foot-square beams spanned the distance between them. Laid over these great beams were 3-inch planks, supporting a slab roof of tabby masonry. On the north were the powder magazine and two big store-rooms. Quarters were along the west curtain, guard-room and chapel on the south, and rooms on the east included a latrine and prison. Altogether there were more than 20 rooms.

The only major work yet to do was beyond the walls. The surrounding moat, 40 feet wide, needed to be deepened, for only part of the moat wall was up to its full 8-foot depth. In fact, of the outworks only the ravelin was finished.

With the fortification this far along, Governor Márquez could give more attention to other busi-ness, such as Lord Cardross' Scottish colony at Port Royal, South Carolina. This was, in the Spanish view, a new and obnoxious settlement that encouraged heathen Indians to raid mission Indians. Further-more, it was in land recognized as Spanish even by the English monarch.

So in September 1686, Márquez sent Captain Alejandro Tomás de Léon, with orders to destroy the colony, which he did. He then sacked and burned Governor Joseph Morton's plantation on Edisto Island.

This cannon tube is typical of most 18th-century guns and bears the cipher of Carlos III, showing it to be Spanish.

This bird's-eye view of Castillo de San Marcos shows how it is laid out and why. The fort was located at the north end of Saint Augustine and on the water for defensive reasons. The moat protected it on four sides, and the Matanzas River lent additional protection as well. The only entrance was at the point closest to the town, so the inhabitants could quickly go to the fort if danger threatened. The fort was designed, too, so that every wall could be seen from some vantage point inside the Castillo. No attacking force could sneak up to the very walls without the defenders seeing them. The original Castillo was simply the exterior walls. Parallel to them were the inner, or courtyard, walls, built also of stone. Beams spanned the space between exterior and inner walls and held up platforms upon which guns sat aimed at the surrounding countryside or out over the water. Such a structure offered scant bombproof defense against incoming projectiles. And the wooden beams were subject to rot in the humid, subtropical air. Work began on stone vaults in 1738 to solve these problems. First, carpenters built wooden forms (see illustration at right) that supported the stone until all pieces of the arch were in place. As the form was removed, other workers began dumping sand, rubble, earth—anything to build up the level—into the spaces above the arches. Over this a cement-like mixture of sand and coquina was placed and tamped down and built up in stages until the desired height was reached. The result was a wide gun platform on top that would support the heaviest guns and provide bombproof spaces beneath.

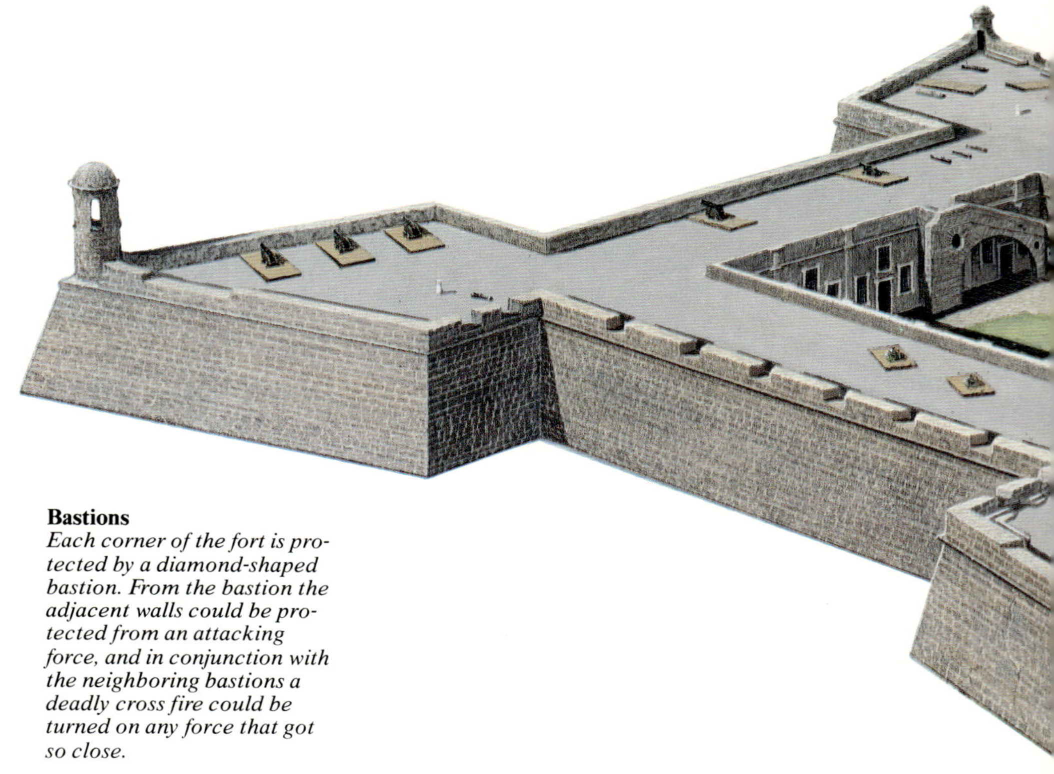

Bastions
Each corner of the fort is protected by a diamond-shaped bastion. From the bastion the adjacent walls could be protected from an attacking force, and in conjunction with the neighboring bastions a deadly cross fire could be turned on any force that got so close.

Guard Rooms

St. Augustine was a garrison town and no one lived inside the Castillo. When soldiers were on guard duty—usually a period of 24 hours—they slept and prepared their meals in these rooms.

Storage Rooms

Most of the rooms around the central courtyard were used for storage. They were stockpiled with gunpowder, ammunition, weapons, lumber, tools, and food, such as beans, rice, flour, and corn, that could be used in time of siege.

Next they set course for Charleston but again, as had happened in 1670, a storm blew them away from the hated English colony. Leon's vessel, the *Rosario,* was lost, and he along with it. Another ship was driven aground, and the last of the little armada limped back to St. Augustine.

Actually the real contest for the southeast was in the backcountry where English traders operated. Governor Márquez sent soldiers and missionaries from St. Augustine to the Apalachecola nation in western Georgia. For the Spaniards, however, it was a losing fight—an exciting, exasperating struggle of diplomacy and intrigue, trade and cupidity, war and religion, slavery and death.

Captain of cuirassiers Diego de Quiroga y Losada assumed the governorship on August 21, 1687, after Márquez fled to Cuba in April. That same day he stopped work on the Castillo because there was no way to feed the workers. These troubles and the certainty of reprisals from the Carolinians sent Capt. Juan de Ayala Escobar directly to Spain for help. He came back with 80 soldiers, the money for maintaining them, and even a Negro slave to help in the fields. The black man, one of a dozen Ayala had hoped to deliver, was a much-needed addition to the colony, and Captain Ayala was welcomed back to St. Augustine with rejoicing "for his good diligence."

Soon there was more black labor for both fields and fortifications. From the Carolina plantations, an occasional slave would slip away and move southward along the waterways. In 1687 a small boat loaded with nine runaways made its way to St. Augustine. The men found work to do and the governor took the two women into his household as servants. It was a fairly happy arrangement: the slaves worked well and soon asked for Catholic baptism.

A few months later, William Dunlop came from Charleston in search of them. Governor Quiroga, reluctant to surrender converted slaves, offered to buy them for the Spanish crown. Dunlop agreed to the sale, even though the governor was as usual short of cash and had given him a promissory note. To seal the bargain, Dunlop gave one of the slaves, a baby girl, her freedom. Later the crown liberated the others.

This incident resulted in a knotty problem. First,

commerce with Carolina, as an English colony, was illegal. Secondly, the crown could not buy freedom for every runaway that came to Florida, as more and more Carolina blacks left their English masters, seeking refuge. The slave issue made any hope of amicable relations between the Spanish and English colonists impossible. Eventually the Spaniards decreed freedom for all Carolina slaves coming to Florida, and the governor established a fortified village—Gracia Real de Mose—for them hardly more than a cannon shot from the Castillo.

Construction work on the Castillo resumed in the spring of 1688, after a shipment of corn came from Apalache. In Havana Governor Quiroga bought for 137 pesos a stone bearing the royal arms to be set into the wall over the gate. At this time, too, the little town entered its "stone age," for as surplus materials from the crown quarries became available, masonry buildings gradually took the place of the board-and-thatch housing that had been traditional here since the founding.

Until the outworks could be finished, the Castillo was vulnerable to siege guns and scaling ladders. Nevertheless it was impossible to push the heavy work of quarrying, lumbering, and hauling at this crucial time. There were too many other pressures. Belatedly trying to counteract English gains and strengthen their own ties with the Indians, the Spaniards built a fort in the Apalachecola country. Unfortunately the soldiers had to be pulled back to St. Augustine when Spain declared war on France in 1689.

This time Spain and England were allies. Yet Governor Quiroga wondered at the presence of English vessels off both northern and southern coasts. As a bit of insurance he wrote a letter telling of a strength far beyond what he had, in the hope that if an English ship would capture the letter they would not know of St. Augustine's weakness. For again the supply situation was critical, and swarms of French corsairs infested the waters between Florida and Havana. Two provision vessels were lost in the Keys and a third fell into French hands. Until food eventually came in from Havana and Campeche, the soldiers had to live on handouts from the townspeople.

To lessen the chances of famine in the future, Florida officials resolved to plant great fields of corn

In the royal arms of Spain, the lions stand for the province of León and the castles for the province of Castile. The shield is surrounded by the chain of the Order of the Golden Fleece, a knightly order founded in 1430, of which the Spanish monarch was grand master. The story of the Golden Fleece recalls the courageous exploits in the ancient Greek myth of Jason and the Argonauts.

The Drawbridge

Pulling up the drawbridge was like locking the door. Once it was pulled up flush against the walls and the portcullis—the heavy grating made of solid yellow pine—rolled shut, no one could get into the fort. To raise the bridge, trapdoors were removed so that the counterweights could descend into the pit. A windlass also lay beneath this trapdoor. Soldiers inserted bars into holes bored into the windlass and rotated it, causing the lifting drums to revolve. The chains, attached to the far end of the bridge, pulled the bridge up as the chains turned on the lifting drums. The counterweights helped neutralize the weight of the bridge so that three soldiers were able to lift its great weight—approximately 1,900 pounds. When the bridge was in the upright position, the soldiers then rolled the portcullis shut behind them, and secured it. This was done every night or in time of danger.

The drawing at left is of the inner workings of the Castillo drawbridge shown in the photograph above.

nearby. And where was better than the broad clearings around the fort? Acres of waving corn soon covered the land almost up to the moat. When the crown heard of these plantings, back to Florida came a royal order banning corn fields within a musket shot of the Castillo. A whole army could hide in the tall corn without being seen by the sentries!

A new governor, Don Laureano de Torres y Ayala, arrived in 1693. At the outset he had to deal with hostilities between St. Augustine and Charleston—hostilities that mocked the Spanish-English alliance in Europe.

More importantly, however, to Governor Torres belongs the credit for completing Castillo de San Marcos. Torres saw the last stones go into place for the water battery—bright yellow coquina that was in contrast to weathered masonry almost a quarter of a century old. In August 1695 the workmen finally moved out of the Castillo to another job: a seawall that would keep storm tides out of the city.

The pile of stone on which Cendoya had planned to spend some 70,000 pesos and which Hita had estimated would cost a good 80,000 if built elsewhere, ended up costing at least 138,375 pesos, a tremendous sum impossible to translate into today's money. But more than the money, it was the blood, sweat, and hardship of the Florida soldier that paid the cost. For the funds came out of money never paid. Let the Castillo be his monument!

And what did completion of this citadel mean? Only a year later, soldiers gaunt with hunger slipped into the church and left an unsigned warning for the governor: If the enemy came, they intended to surrender, for they were starving.

Defending San Marcos

The test of the Castillo's strength was not long in coming. Relations with France had become peaceful, but incursions by the English-led Indians kept the backcountry inflamed. As tensions increased, Gov. José de Zúñiga y Cerda looked at the St. Augustine defenses with an experienced eye. Zúñiga knew, after a military career spanning 28 years, that strong walls were not enough. The Castillo's guns were ancient and obsolete—many of them unserviceable. The powder from México so fouled the gun barrels that after "four shots, the Ball would not go in the Cannon." Arquebuses, muskets, powder, and shot were in short supply.

Once again Captain Ayala sailed directly to Spain to ask for aid. It was a race against time, for the War of the Spanish Succession with France and Spain allied against England had broken out. Gov. James Moore of Carolina lost no time moving against St. Augustine in 1702. If he could capture the Castillo, he would clap an English lock on the Straits of Florida and forestall a possible Spanish-French attack on Charleston.

On the way south, Moore's forces destroyed the Franciscan missions in the Guale country. At St. Augustine they avoided the Castillo and occupied the town, whose inhabitants had fled to the fort. South and west of its walls, where the town approached the fort, the Spaniards burned many structures that could have hidden the enemy advance.

Moore's 500 Englishmen and 300 Indians vastly outnumbered the 230 soldiers and 180 Indians and Negroes in the Castillo's garrison, but Moore was ill-equipped to besiege the Castillo. He settled down to await the arrival of more artillery from Jamaica, and thus matters stood when four Spanish men-of-war arrived and blocked the harbor entrance, bottling up Moore's fleet of eight small vessels. Moore burned his ships, left most of his supplies, and retreated overland to the St. Johns River. He left St.

Augustine in ashes, but the Castillo and its people survived.

The ease with which the English had taken and held the city for almost two months made it clear that more defenses were needed. Moreover, English and Indian obliteration of the missions in Apalache, Timucua, and Guale had reduced Spanish control to the tiny area directly under the Castillo guns.

In the next two decades strong earthworks and palisades, buttressed at strategic points with redoubts, made St. Augustine a walled town, secure as long as there were enough soldiers to man the walls. But in those dark days who could be sure of tomorrow? In 1712 came *La Gran Hambre*—the Great Hunger—when starving people even ate the dogs and cats.

At last the war ended in 1714. The threat to St. Augustine lessened, but it was an uneasy kind of peace with many "incidents." In 1728 Col. William Palmer of Carolina marched against the presidio. The grim walls of the fort, the readiness of the heavy guns, and the needle-sharp points of the yucca plants lining the palisades were a powerful deterrent. Palmer "refrained" from taking the town. For their part, the Spaniards fired their guns, but made no sorties.

Palmer's bold foray to the very gates of St. Augustine foreshadowed a new move southward by the English, beginning with the settlement of Savannah in 1732. With his eye on Florida, James Oglethorpe landed at St. Simons Island in 1736, built Fort Frederica, and nurtured it into a strong military post. From Frederica he pushed his Georgia boundary southward all the way to the St. Johns River—a scant 35 miles from St Augustine.

Meanwhile, Castillo de San Marcos began to show signs of being 50 years old. The capable engineer and frontier diplomat Antonio de Arredondo came from Havana to inspect Florida's defenses and make recommendations. Backed by Arredondo's expertise, Gov. Manuel de Montiano wrote a frank letter to the governor of Cuba, who was now responsible for Florida's security: "Your Excellency must know that this castle, the only defense here, has no bombproofs for the protection of the garrison, that the counterscarp is too low, that there is no covered way, that the curtains are without demilunes, that there are no other exterior works to give them time for a

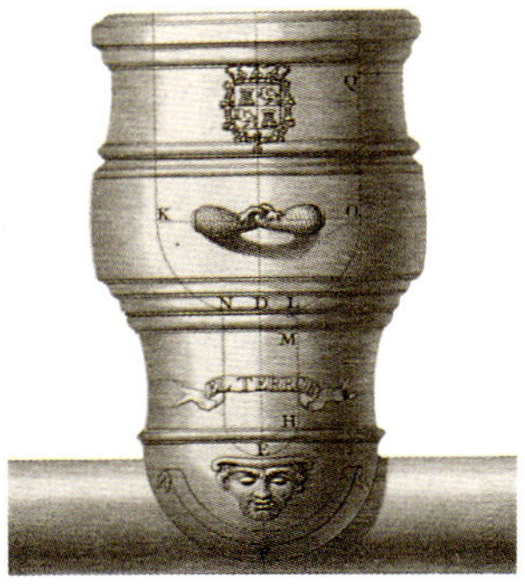

Mortars have long held an important place in the family of field artillery because of their ability to throw a projectile over a barrier. The Spaniards were among the earliest to use mortars whose trajectory could be varied, thereby making the mortars even more effective.

Spanish-English Conflict, 1670-1748

Selected attacks
English
Spanish
French

Settlement
English to 1700
English after 1700
Spanish

The Treaty of Madrid, 1670, aimed at stopping the Spanish-English contest along the South Atlantic coast by confirming Spanish claims as far north as 32°30'. The English agreed to this but within a few years continued their push southward. Savannah, settled in 1733, was well within Spanish territory.

CAROLINA

Charleston
1670, 1706
1706

Edisto Island, 1706

Port Royal, 1686

Savannah

Savannah

32°30'N
Treaty of Madrid, 1670

Altamaha

Santa Catalina Island, 1680

GUALE COUNTRY

Fort King George

Fort Frederica, 1742

St. Simons Island, 1742

GEORGIA

Flint

Atlantic Ocean

St. Marys

Suwannee

Santa Maria Island, 1683

San Juan de Puerto, 1683

St. Johns

Fort San Diego, 1740

San Carlos, 1693

San Pedro de Patale, 1704

Ayubale, 1704

St. Augustine,
1683, 1702, 1728, 1740

Anastasia Island

San Luis
de Talimali

Acuilla

TIMUCUA

Matanzas Inlet,
1683, 1740, 1741, 1742, 1743

APALACHE

San Juan
de Guacara,
1693

Santa Catalina
de Afuica,
1685

Santa Fe, 1702

Little Matanzas
Inlet, 1686

Apalachicola

Apalache Fort,
1677, 1682

Apalachee Bay

Mosquito Inlet,
1682

Cape
San Blas

FLORIDA

Gulf of Mexico

North

0   50   100 Kilometers

0   50   100 Miles

Tampa Bay

Kissimmee

The most serious attack on the Castillo took place when James Oglethorpe, the founder of Georgia, arrived off Saint Augustine on June 13, 1740, with 7 warships and 1,400 troops. Oglethorpe's arrival was not entirely unexpected. The English and Spaniards were rivals in Europe and continued their contest in the New World, with the Spaniards becoming increasingly restive as the English penetrated into the lands south of Charleston. By the time Oglethorpe arrived in Georgia, only about 150 miles north of the Castillo and on land the Spaniards considered their own, tensions were high. Oglethorpe wanted to guarantee that his new settlements would be secure from Spanish attack, so he decided to capture and occupy Spain's base in Florida—before they decided to attack him. Oglethorpe had his work cut out for him, because the Castillo was superbly sited. Creeks and marshes protected it to the west and south. On the east the bay stretched to a shallow bar across the harbor entrance that kept heavy warships out of range. The only land approach was from the north. An English spy for Oglethorpe reported that the fort was well supplied and staffed. There were "22 pieces of Cannon well mounted on the Bastions from 6 pound'rs to 36.... There is a guard of a Lieutenant, a Serjeant & 2 Corporals & 30 Soldiers here who is relieved Every Day.... There is a Mote Round it of 30 foot wide & a draw Bridge of about 15 foot long, they draw every Night &

Lett it down in the Morning." With this kind of information Oglethorpe knew what he was up against and came prepared. Fortunately for the defenders, the attackers were divided. Some had landed on Vilano Point and on Anastasia Island, opposite the Castillo and were setting up batteries there. Some troops were on the mainland where they had seized vacant Fort Mose, a free black settlement just north of the Castillo. Though the total British force outnumbered the defenders, Gov. Manuel de Montiano reasoned that his forces could attack one segment before it could be reinforced by the other two. This is exactly what the Spaniards did, overwhelming the British force at Fort Mose. Undecided about further land attack, the British then began shelling the Castillo and the town from their siege batteries in a bombardment that lasted 27 days. But the British mortars and siege guns were too far away to be totally effective and the damage they did was slight. Some of the newer stonework was damaged. Only two Spanish soldiers were killed during the attack and another had a leg shot away. Among the British there was no agreement regarding another course of action. Oglethorpe himself was down with a fever, and the troops had become unnecessarily tired by purposeless maneuvering. With the approach of the hurricane season, the naval commander refused to continue the blockade, and British forces left. The Castillo and its defenders had done what they were meant to do.

long defense; ... we are as bare outside as we are without life inside, for there are no guns that could last 24 hours and if there were, we have no artillerymen to serve them."

Cuba's governor was a resourceful administrator eager to meet his responsibilities. He sent guns, soldiers, artisans, convicts, provisions, and money. The walls would be raised five feet and masonry vaults, to withstand English bombs, would replace the rotting beams of old rooms in the Castillo. Stronger outworks would be built, too. To supervise the project, Engineer Pedro Ruiz de Olano came from Venezuela. The work began in April 1738 rather inauspiciously. The master of construction, one Cantillo, was a syphilitic too sick to earn his 16-*real* daily wage. Much of his work fell to his assistant, a 12-*real* master mason. All six stonecutters were Negroes. One was an invalid, and none of them as yet had much skill with coquina. For moving stone, there was but one oxcart. The labor gang—52 convicts—was too small. Nevertheless, quarry and kiln hummed with activity, and in the Castillo the crash of demolition echoed as the convicts pulled down old structures and began trenching for the new bombproofs. They started on the east, because this side faced the inlet where enemy action was likely.

As usual, misfortunes beset the work. Cantillo's illness worsened and Blas de Ortega came from Havana to replace him. Eight convicts working at the limekiln deserted. Engineer Ruiz moved a crew of carpenters, sawyers, and axemen from work on the Castillo to rebuild a blockhouse where the trail to Apalache crossed the St. Johns River.

The oxcart driver broke his arm. Quarrying and stonecutting dragged. The old quarry played out. Luckily, a new one was found and opened, even though farther away. And Havana sent two more carts and more stonecutters and convicts.

It was well into October before the carpenters began setting the forms for the vaults. The masons followed close on their heels and finished the first of the massive, round-arched bombproofs before the year ended. Just a year later all eight vaults, side by side along the east curtain, were done. Each one spanned a 17- by 34-foot area, and had its own door to the courtyard. Windows above and beside the door let in light and air.

Forts are often described with words like impregnable, un-assailable, grim, invulnerable, and redoubtable. These descriptions often came about because of their armaments. A strategically positioned fort with a full complement of weaponry would be a problem for any invader, because the fortress, unlike naval ships, provided a stable platform upon which guns could be mounted and trained on the enemy. Anyone approaching within approximately 500 yards would be in great danger, even though the artillery in those times was not always accurate and aim was extremely difficult.

Basically all artillery falls into two categories: mortars and guns. Mortars were designed to fire the largest and heaviest projectiles on a curved trajectory. They could shoot over obstacles or fortifications, landing on, and perhaps piercing, the deck of a ship, or hitting a pile of powder kegs or other supplies behind fortified walls, or just wreaking havoc and demoralizing the people. Guns fired their projectiles in a flat trajectory, and their effectiveness in turn depended upon the weight of the shot: the greater the weight of the shot, the greater the muzzle velocity—the speed at which the shot exited the gun—and the farther the shot would go and the deadlier it would be.

The first artillery pieces were made of forged iron. The greatest concern was in producing a weapon that could contain

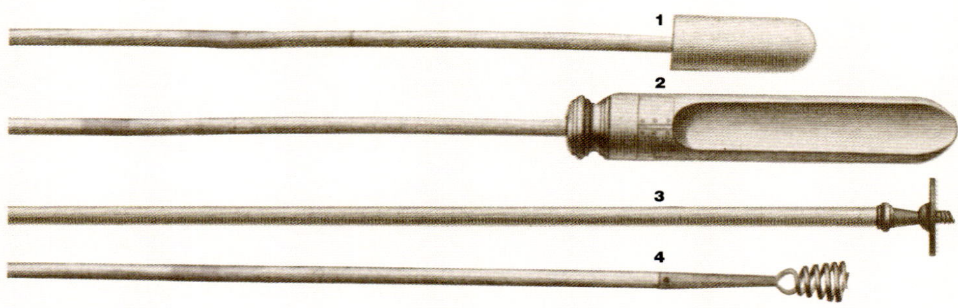

1. Sponge
2. Powder ladle
3. Scraper
4. Worm
5. 24-pounder cannon
6. 16-pounder cannon
7. 12-pounder cannon
8. Grape shot, side view
9. Tongs for handling hot shot
10. Garrison carriage, top view
11. Garrison carriage, side view

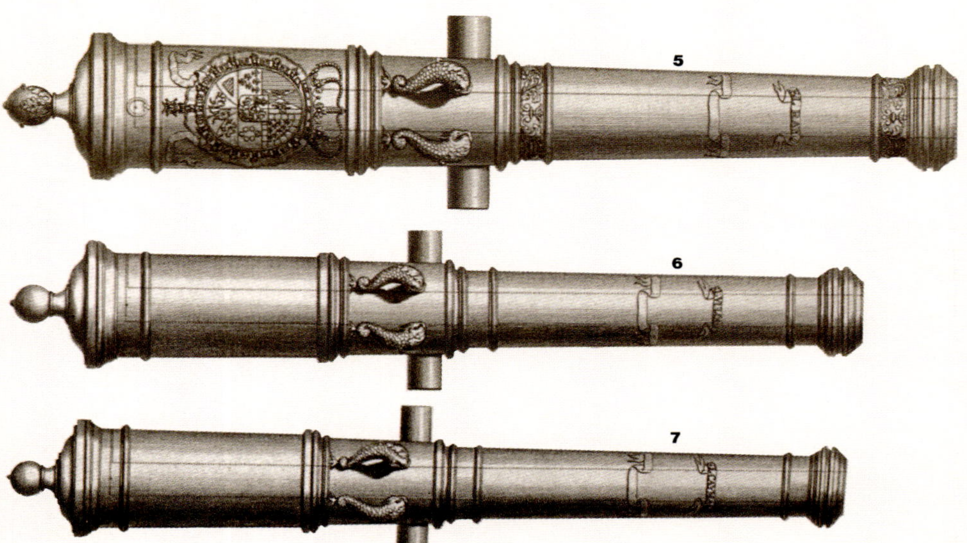

the explosive force of the gun-powder, hurl the projectile at the enemy, and not blow up in the faces of the gun crew. Once guns could be cast in a single piece in either brass or bronze, great strides were made in the effectiveness of the artillery pieces. By the 18th century bronze seems to have been the metal of choice. The guns and mortars were highly decorated. All bore the coat of arms of the sovereign. Usually the maker was identified in some way; the name might be part of the base ring or shown in a cipher below the sovereign's arms. Garlands of flowers, animals, and mythical creatures sometimes decorated the piece. All Spanish guns were named—*Vindicator, Invincible, Destroyer* are a few examples—and the authorities made sure that each gun's whereabouts was always known. This has been invaluable for present-day historians investigating what guns were used where and when. Guns were classified by the weight of the projectile: a 12-pounder gun shot a 12-pound ball. The kinds of projectiles varied greatly: solid shot, canister shot (a container full of bullets), grape shot (cloth container full of bullets), and bombs or grenades (hollow shot filled with gunpowder) fired from a mortar. Sometimes solid shot was heated until it was red hot. If it landed on a ship, hot shot could set a wooden ship afire. Ordnance enabled a fortification to meet the potential the military engineers had hoped for when they sited and built it.

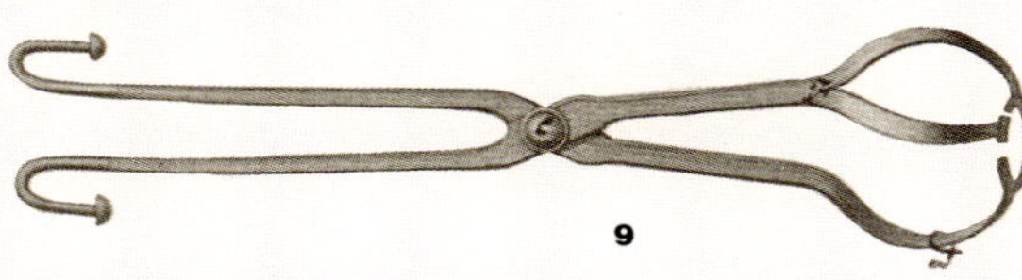

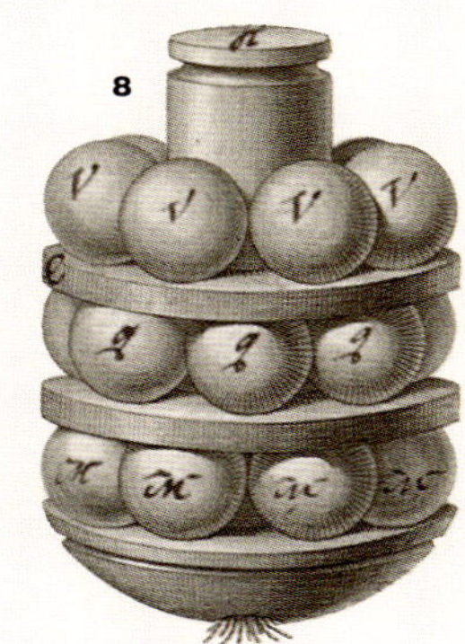

Tools for Guns

The tools used to operate the ordnance had a variety of functions. The wet sponge swabbed out the cannon to make sure all sparks were extinguished. The ladle dumped the exact amount of powder needed into the chamber. The scraper removed any powder residue. The worm removed unfired bits of cartridge and wadding. The point was to make sure the cannon was clean before it was loaded and fired.

These illustrations come from Tomás de Morla's A Treatise on Artillery, *a 4-volume work published in Madrid in 1803.*

The tops of the ponderous vaults were leveled off with a fill of coquina chips and sand. Tabby mortar was poured onto the surface, and tampers beat the mixture smooth. After the first layer set, others were added until the pavement was six inches thick. The whole roof was thus made into a gun deck, and cannon were no longer restricted to the bastions alone. For unlike the old raftered roof, the new terreplein was buttressed by construction that could take tremendous weight and terrific shock; and masonry four feet thick protected the rooms underneath from bombardment. In San Carlos bastion, by mid-January of 1740, they had finished the tall watchtower and the new parapet.

It was the English settlement of Georgia that had spurred all this activity. In fact, Spain's plan for recovery of Georgia and other Spanish-claimed land was well past the first stages. Troops were assembling in Havana and reinforcements of 400 had already come to Florida. The situation came to a head when Spanish officials boarded Capt. Robert Jenkins' ship *Rebecca*, believing the English mariners to be illegally carrying goods to Spanish settlements, an enterprise forbidden by Spanish law. In the ensuing scuffle, Jenkins' ear was sliced off. Jenkins, back in London, reported to Parliament that the Spanish officer who handed him back his ear said: "Carry it to your King and tell his majesty that if he were present I would serve him in the same manner."

Alexander Pope, the couplet maker, smiled and said: "The Spaniards did a waggish thing/Who cropped our ears and sent them to the King." But others were not amused, and England and Spain declared war in 1739. It was called, of course, the War of Jenkins' Ear.

England's main target was the Caribbean, with Havana at center with Portobelo, Cartagena, and St. Augustine on the perimeter. Admiral Edward Vernon quickly won fame with his capture of Portobelo in 1739. Oglethorpe tried to imitate him in Florida. Already he had probed the St. Johns River approaches; St. Augustine would be next.

Governor Montiano, however, was fully aware of weaknesses. "Considering that 21 months have been spent on a bastion and eight arches," he pointed out, "we need at least eight years for rehabilitation of the Castillo."

46

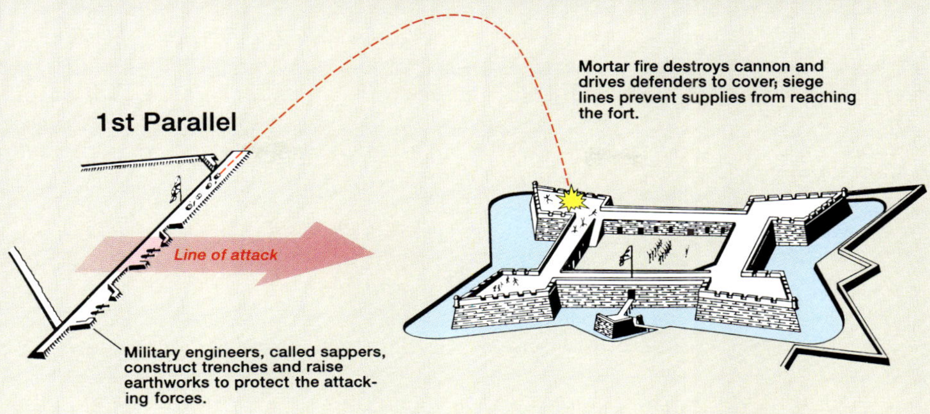

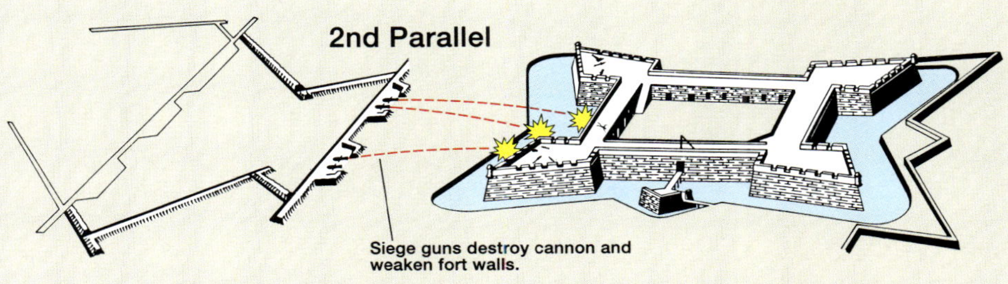

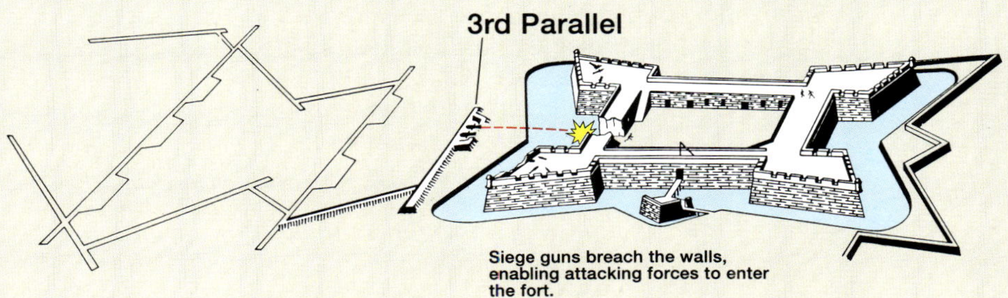

A Fort's Defenses

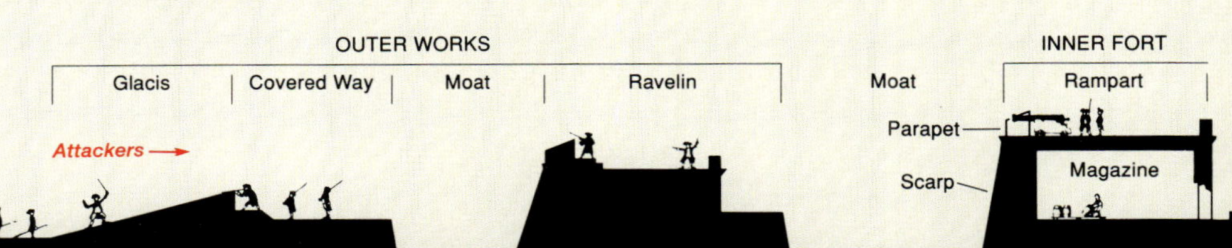

The Cubo Line originally stretched from the Castillo to the San Sebastián River. It was strengthened and rebuilt repeatedly by both the Spaniards and the British. The city gate, a part of the line, was built in 1808, only a few years before the United States took control of Florida.

His concerns were genuine, for work on the vaults had to stop as the war dried up construction funds. The fort was left in a strangely irregular shape. The east side, including San Carlos bastion, was at the new height, but all others were several feet lower. The old rooms still lined three sides of the courtyard.

On June 13, 1740, seven British warships dropped anchor outside the inlet. The long-expected siege of St. Augustine had begun. Montiano hastily sent the news to Havana and with it a plea for help. He had 750 soldiers and the 120 or more sailors who manned the galliots. Rations would last only until the end of June.

The attackers numbered almost 1,400, including sailors and Indian allies. While the warships blockaded the harbor on the east, William Palmer came in from the north with a company of Highlanders and occupied the deserted outpost called Fort Mose. Oglethorpe landed his men and guns on each side of the inlet and began building batteries across the bay from the Castillo.

Montiano saw at once that all the English positions were separated from each other by water and could not speedily reinforce one another. Fort Mose, at the village of the black runaways a couple of miles north of the Castillo, was the weakest. At dawn on June 26 a sortie from St. Augustine hit Fort Mose, and in the bloodiest action of the siege scattered the Highlanders and burned the palisaded fortification. Colonel Palmer, veteran of Florida campaigns, was among the dead.

As if in revenge, the siege guns at the inlet opened fire. Round shot whistled low over the bay and crashed into fort and town. Bombs from the mortars soared high—deadly dots against the bright summer sky—and fell swiftly to burst with terrific concussion. The townspeople fled, 2,000 of them, some to the woods, others to the covered way where Castillo walls screened them from the shelling.

For 27 nerve-shattering days the British batteries thundered. At the Castillo, newly laid stones in the east parapet scattered under the hits, but the weathered old walls held strong. As one Englishman observed, the native rock "will not splinter but will give way to cannon ball as though you would stick a knife into cheese." One of the balls shot away a gunner's leg, but only two men in the Castillo were killed during the bombardment.

The heavy guns of San Marcos and the long 9-pounders of the fast little galliots in the harbor kept the British back. Despite the bluster of the cannonades, the siege had stalemated. Astride the inlet, Oglethorpe and his men battled insects and shifting sand on barren, sun-baked shores, while Spanish soldiers in San Marcos, down to half rations themselves, saw their families and friends starving. On July 6 Montiano wrote, "My greatest anxiety is provisions. If these do not come, there is no doubt that we shall die in the hands of hunger."

The very next day came news that supplies had reached a harbor down the coast south of Matanzas. Shallow-draft Spanish vessels went down the waterway behind Anastasia Island, fought their way out through Matanzas Inlet and, hugging the coast, went to fetch the provisions. Coming back into Matanzas that same night, they found the British blockade gone; they reached St. Augustine unopposed.

Oglethorpe made ready to assault the Castillo despite the low morale of his men. His naval commander, however, was nervous over the approach of the hurricane season and refused to cooperate. Without support from the warships, Oglethorpe had to withdraw. Daybreak on July 20—38 days since the British had arrived at St. Augustine—revealed that the redcoats were gone.

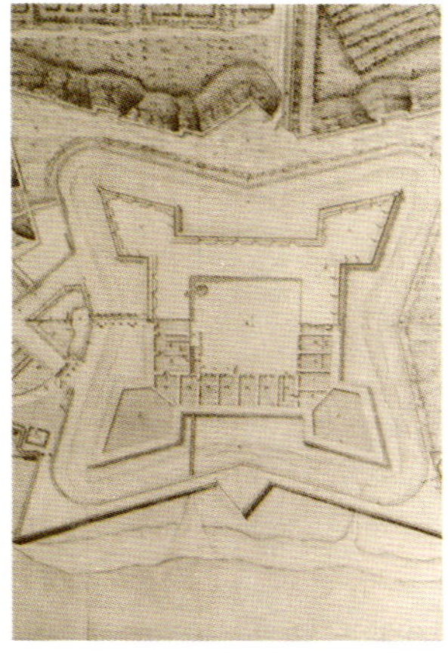

This 1763 engraving shows the finished Castillo after all the bombproof vaults and a new ravelin had been built.

Léctio Epístolæ beáti Pauli Apóstoli ad Colossénses.

Colof. 1.

Fratres : Si consurrexístis cũ Christo, quæ sursũ sunt quærite, ubi Christus est in déxtera Dei sedens : quæ sursum sunt sápite, non quæ super terrã. Mórtui enim estis, & vita vestra abscóndita est cum Christo in Deo. Cùm Christus apparúerit, vita vestra : tunc & vos apparébitis cum ipso in glória.

Finita Epístola Celebrans incipit.

Alle   lú   ja.

Et totum decantat ter, elevando vocem gradatim : & Chorus post quamlibet vicem, in eodem tono repetit illud idem. Posteà Chorus prosequitur, ℣. Confitémini Dómino, quóniam bonus : quóniã in sæculum misericórdia ejus.

Psal. 117.

Deinde dicitur Tractus.

Psal. 116.

Laudáte Dóminum omnes Gentes : & collaudáte eum omnes pópuli. ℣. Quóniam confirmáta est super nos misericórdia ejus : & véritas Dómini manet in ætérnum.

Ad Evangelium non portantur luminaria, sed tantùm incensũ : petitur benedíctio, & alia fiunt de more.

Sequéntia sancti Evangélij se-

nit María Magdaléne, & áltera María, vidére sepúlchrum. Et ecce terræ môtus factus est magnus. Angelus enim Dómini descéndit de cælo : & accédens revólvit lápidem, & sedêbat super eum : erat autem aspéctus ejus sicut fulgur : & vestiméntũ ejus sicut nix. Præ timôre autẽ ejus extérriti sunt custódes, & facti sunt velut mórtui. Respóndens autem Angelus dixit muliéribus: Nolîte timére vos : scio enim, quòd Jesum, qui crucifíxus est, quæritis : Non est hîc : Surrêxit enim sicut dixit. Venîte, & vidête locum, ubi pósitus erat Dóminus. Et citò eúntes, dícite discípulis ejus, quia surréxit. Et ecce præcêdit vos in Galilæã : ibi eum vidébitis. Ecce prædíxi vobis.

Non dicitur Credo, sed finito Evangelio Sacerdos dicit: Dóminus vobíscum. Posteà Orêmus. Non dicitur Offertorium. Ad Lavábo, dicitur Glória Patri. Secreta.

Suscipe, quæsumus Dómine, preces pópuli tui, cum oblatiónibus hostiárum : ut Paschálibus initiáta mystérijs, ad æternitátis nobis medêlam, te operánte profíciant. Per Dóminum.

Præfatio. Te quidem Dómine omni témpore, sed in hac potíssimũ nocte. ut infrà in Canone.

Infra actiónem.

The End of an Era

Beyond the military aspects, which were so vital to the decision to establish St. Augustine, the city had become a vibrant community of soldiers, their families, government officials, and shopkeepers. Religion and the church played an important part in the life of the community. This page from a Roman Catholic missal, printed in 1690, is open to the service for Easter. The right-hand column recounts the story of how the Marys went to the tomb and found it empty.

This was why the Castillo had been built—to resist aggression, to stand firm through the darkest hour. Years of dogged labor and privations had brought the Castillo to the point where it could easily withstand a siege. Yet it remained unfinished, while in 1742 Spanish forces from Havana and St. Augustine tried unsuccessfully to take Oglethorpe's settlement at Fort Frederica. The next year Oglethorpe moved unsuccessfully against St. Augustine.

Work still needed to be done on the vaults, but other projects were even more urgent. First, came repair of the bombardment damage. After that, the defenses around fort and town were strengthened and a strong new earth wall called the hornwork was thrown up across the land approach, half a mile north of town. And for a year or more a sizable crew was busy at Matanzas building a permanent tower and battery, since the events of 1740 had again shown the vital defensive importance of this inlet a few miles south of St. Augustine.

Several years slipped by with nothing being done to Castillo itself, the heart of the defense system. Termites and rot were in the old rafters, and in 1749 part of the roof collapsed.

The governor's appeal to the crown eventually brought action. Engineer Pedro de Brozas y Garay came from Ceuta in Africa to replace Ruiz, who was returning to Spain. Having overseen the construction of the last fort rooms, it was Brozas who, with Governor Alonso Fernández de Heredia, stood under the royal coat of arms at the sally port as the masons set in the inscription giving credit to the governor and himself for completion of the Castillo in 1756. The ceremony was a politic gesture, carried out on the name day of King Fernando VI; but in truth there was still a great deal to do.

The new bombproof vaults had raised the Castillo's walls by five feet. Where once they had measured about 25 feet from foundation to crown of parapet,

This British musket dates from 1777-90 and is of the type that would have been used by the British forces stationed at the Castillo from 1763 to 1784. It is 4 feet, 8 inches long.

now they were more than 30. The little ravelin of 1682 could no longer shield the main gate, and as yet the covered way screened only the base of the high new walls. The glacis existed only on the plans.

So, having finished the vaults, the builders moved outside and worked until money ran out in the spring of 1758. The break lasted until 1762, by which time Britain and Spain were again at war. Spain, as an ally of France, got into the fracas just at the time when Britain had eliminated France as a factor in the control of North America and was quite ready to take on Spain. And this time the British would capture the pearl of the Antilles—Havana itself.

Havana was well fortified, and the general officers sitting there were perhaps more worried about St. Augustine than Havana. They released 10,000 pesos for strengthening the Florida fortifications and sent Engineer Pablo Castelló, who had been teaching mathematics at the military college in Havana, to assist the ailing Pedro Brozas.

St. Augustine had only 25 convicts for labor, but when work began on July 27, 1762, many soldiers and townspeople sensed the urgency, for Havana was already besieged, and volunteered to help. Since much of the project was a simple but strenuous task of digging and moving a mountain of sand from borrow pit to earthwork, all able-bodied people were welcome. The volunteers did, in fact, contribute labor worth more than 12,000 pesos. The only paid workers were the teamsters driving the 50 horses that hauled the fill. Each dray dumped 40 cubic feet of earth, and the hauling kept on until the covered way had been raised five more feet to its new height.

The masons soon finished a stone parapet, six feet high, for the new covered way. With this wall in place, the teamsters moved outside the covered way and began dumping fill for the glacis. This simple but important structure was a carefully designed slope from the field up to the parapet of the covered way. Not only would it screen the main walls and covered way, but its upward slope would lift attackers right into the sights of the fort cannon.

Meanwhile, to replace the 1682 ravelin, Castelló began a new one with room for five cannon and a powder magazine. He realigned the moat wall to accommodate the larger work and pushed the job along so that as December of 1762 ended, the masons laid the final stone of the cordon for the ravelin. They never started its parapet, for the close of the year brought the devastating news that Spain would give Florida to Great Britain.

So Spain's work on the fort ended. And although ravelin and glacis were not finished, Castillo de San Marcos was a handsome structure. The main walls were finished with a hard, waterproofing, lime plaster, shining white in the sunlight with the brilliance of Spain's olden glory. In the haste of building, engineers had not forgotten such niceties as classic molded cornices, pendants, and pilasters to cast relieving shadows on stark smooth walls. At the point of each bastion was color—the tile-red plaster of the sentry boxes. White and red. These were Spain's symbolic colors, revealed again in the banner floating above the ramparts.

With walls high over the blue waters of the bay, its towers thrusting toward the clouds, and guns of bright bronze or iron pointed over turf and sweep of marsh toward the gloom of the forest or the distant surf breaking on the bar, San Marcos was properly the background for Florida's capital. In the narrow streets that led to the citadel, military men and sailors mingled with tradesman and townsfolk. Indians, their nakedness smeared with beargrease against the bugs, were a strange contrast to the silken opulence of the governor's lady. But this was St. Augustine—a town of contrasts, with a long past and an uncertain future.

The day of the transfer to British rule was July 21, 1763. At Castillo de San Marcos, Gov. Melchor de Feliú delivered the keys to Maj. John Hedges, at the moment the ranking representative of George III. The Spanish troops departed Florida, and with them went the entire Spanish population. The English were left with an empty city.

The defenses they found at St. Augustine were far stronger than the ones that had stopped Oglethorpe in 1740. The renovated Castillo, which the new owners called Fort St. Mark, was the citadel of a defense-in-depth system that began with fortified towers at St. Augustine and Matanzas inlets and blockhouses at the St. Johns River crossings. Since St. Augustine was on a small peninsula with Matanzas Bay on one side and the San Sebastián River on the other, there was only one way to reach the city by land; and Fort Mose, rebuilt and enlarged after 1740, guarded this lone access. In 1762 Mose also became the anchor for a mile-long defense line across the peninsula to a strong redoubt on the San Sebastián. This earthwork, planted at its base with prickly pear, protected the farmlands behind it. Just north of the Castillo, the hornwork spanned the narrowest part of the peninsula. A third line stretched from the Castillo to the San Sebastián, and this one was intersected by a fourth line that enclosed the town on west and south. Along the eastern shore was the stone seawall. One by one, these defenses had evolved in the years after 1702.

Such defensive precautions seemed outmoded, now that all eastern North America was under one sovereignty. Obviously the old enmities between Florida and the English colonies had departed with the Spaniards; Britain saw no need for concern about the fortifications. No need, that is, until the Thirteen Colonies showed disquieting signs of rebellion. And as rebellion flamed into revolution, St. Augustine entered a new role as capital of George III's loyal province of East Florida.

In the summer of 1775, after Lexington and Concord, British concerns about the Castillo's state of repair could be seen. The gate was repaired and the well in the courtyard, which had become brackish, was re-dug. In several of the high-arched bomb-proofs, the carpenters doubled the capacity by building a second floor, for St. Augustine was regimental headquarters and many redcoated troops were quartered in Fort St. Mark.

By October 1776 the British had renovated two of the three lines constructed north of the city by the Spaniards. In place of the old earthwork that hemmed in the town on the south and west, however, they depended on a pair of detached redoubts at the San Sebastián, one at the ford and the other at the ferry. Later they added five other redoubts in the same quadrant. Many improvements were made to the outer works as well.

Behind the thick walls of the fort were stored weapons and equipment that went to arm British forces for repeated use against the rebellious colonials to the north. The damp prison also held a number of these colonists.

Bottle body

Plate fragment, majolica

Dish fragment, majolica

Dish with caduceus (medical symbol)

Spanish olive jar

Platter base fragment, slipware

China accordion player

Bowl fragment, pearlware-mochaware

Even as the British were working to secure the Castillo against a possible attack, international events brought Spain back into the picture. In 1779 Spain declared war on Britain after France promised help in retrieving Florida, if the powers allied against Britain were victorious. One Spanish plan even had the Spaniards launching a surprise attack on the Castillo: Troops would sail upriver from Matanzas, land south of town, sweep north through St. Augustine, and take the Castillo by storm. If this failed they would settle in for a siege. At the last minute, practically, the authorities decided to attack Pensacola, on Florida's Gulf Coast, instead. A Spanish attack on the British inside a fortress designed and built by Spanish engineers would have been full of irony.

In the settlement after the Revolution, the Spaniards did indeed recover Florida, and on July 12, 1784, the transfer took place.

The Spaniards returned to an impossible situation. The border problems of earlier times had multiplied as runaway slaves from Georgia found welcome among the Seminole Indians, and ruffians from both land and sea made Florida their habitat.

Bedeviled by these perversities and distracted by revolutionary unrest in Latin America, Spain nevertheless did what had to be done at the Castillo—repairs to the bridges, a new pine stairway for San Carlos tower, a bench for the criminals in the prison. In 1785 Mariano de la Rocque designed an attractive entrance in the neoclassic style for the chapel doorway. It was built, only to crumble slowly away like the Spanish hold on Florida.

Defense strategies had changed too, over the years. The British had built a few redoubts to cover vulnerable approaches on the west and south. The Spaniards on their return adapted the British works but also greatly strengthened the long wall from the Castillo to the San Sebastián River. They widened its moat to 40 feet, lined the entire length of the 9-foot-high earthwork with palm logs, and planted it with prickly pear. The three redoubts were armed with light cannon, and a new city gate was completed in 1808. Its twin towers of white masonry were trimmed with red plaster, and each roof was capped with a pomegranate, a symbol of fertility.

Even though San Marcos remained a bulwark against American advances, Florida had lost its former importance to Spain as independence movements sprang up in one South American Spanish colony after another. Constant pressure from the expanding United States finally resulted in Spain's ceding Florida to the United States. Perhaps Spanish officials signed the papers with a sigh of relief, glad to be rid of a province so burdensome and unprofitable for 300 years. On July 10, 1821, the ensign of Spain fluttered down to the thunderous salute of Castillo cannon, and the 23-star flag of the United States of America was hauled aloft.

In this new era, the aging fort was already a relic. Fortunately for its preservation, the U.S. strategy for coastal defense did not require much alteration of the Castillo. U.S. Army engineers added only a water battery in the east moat, mounted a few new guns on the bastions, and improved the glacis during the 1840s.

The fort's name was also changed, for the Americans chose to honor Gen. Francis Marion, Revolutionary leader and son of the very colony against whose possible aggression San Marcos had been built. Congress restored the original name in 1942, almost 20 years after the fort had been designated a national monument.

Heavy doors and iron bars that once protected precious stores of food and ammunition made the old fort a good prison, and the prison days soon obscured the olden times when Spain's hold upon Florida depended upon the strength of these walls and the brave hearts that served here.

Now the echo of the Spanish tongue has faded and the scarred walls are silent. The records tell of the people who built and defended the Castillo—and those who attacked it, too. In the archives are countless instances of unselfish zeal and loyalty, the cases of Ransom, Collins, and Carr, the crown's patriarchal protection of its Indian vassals, the unflagging work of the friars. The structure itself tells its own story. As William Cullen Bryant, 19th-century poet wrote: "The old fort of St. Mark is a noble work, frowning over the Matanzas, and it is worth making a long journey to see."

The Spanish government constructed replicas of Christopher Columbus' three ships to commemorate the 500th anniversary of his voyage to America. The ships followed Columbus' route across the Atlantic and made calls at ports throughout the Americas. Here the Santa Maria, *in the foreground,* Pinta, *and* Niña *visit St. Augustine in 1992.*

Guide and Adviser

St. Augustine is the oldest, continuously inhabited city founded by Europeans in the present-day United States. It represents the beginnings of contact between Spanish settlers and the native inhabitants, the emergence of the Hispanic American, the struggle between Spanish, French, and English settlers for control of the southeastern Atlantic coast, and ultimately the birth of the United States.

Visiting St. Augustine

As well as being an old city, with many historic houses on quiet, narrow streets, St. Augustine is a bustling modern city with a range of facilities and accommodations to meet all expectations and travel budgets.

Begin your visit to the city at the Visitor Information Center on San Marco Avenue, opposite the Castillo. Here you can get free information, maps, and answers to your questions from the staff. The center is open daily from 8 a.m. to 5:30 p.m. Limited parking is available for patrons. You may write: Visitor Information Center, P.O. Drawer 210, St. Augustine, FL 32085; or call 904-825-1000. Additional information is available from the St. Augustine and St. Johns County Chamber of Commerce, 1 Ribera Street, St. Augustine, FL 320841 or call 904-829-5681.

St. Augustine is a wonderful city to walk in, for it is compact and easy to find your way around. Take time to leave the main streets and walk through residential areas to get a feel for the city and the way it was laid out. St. Augustine has its own personality and charm that distinguish it from such other colonial communities as Williamsburg, Charleston, and Santa Fe. Today's St. Augustine bears the imprint of Henry Flagler (1830-1913), a close partner of John D. Rockefeller in the development of the Standard Oil Company and a railroad tycoon in Florida. Flagler bought several small railroads in Florida, consolidated them, and laid track that eventually ran from Jacksonville to Key West. Along with his railroad he built luxury hotels in Daytona, Palm Beach, Miami, and St. Augustine and helped to create the tourist industry that has played such an important role in Florida's economy in the 20th century. Flagler's legacy lives on in St. Augustine where Flagler College occupies the former Hotel Ponce de Leon at Cordova and King streets and in the Lightner Museum housed in the old Alcazar Hotel across the street from the college. The St. John's County Courthouse and the St. Augustine City Hall also occupy Flagler buildings. Flagler is buried on the grounds of the Flagler Memorial Presbyterian Church.

St. George Street, a pedestrian walkway between Castillo Drive and Cathedral Place, is lined with shops and restaurants of every type and description. The **Spanish Quarter,** a restored 18th-century portion of the city, is a living history museum operated by the state of Florida on the north end of St. George Street. Along this street a number of residences dating back more than two centuries have either been reconstructed or restored by the St. Augustine Restoration and Preservation Commission. Some of them may be open to the public. But do not assume that they are. Inquire at the Visitor Information Center for specific information about opening and closing times.

The Oldest House, located at the corner of St. Francis and Charlotte streets, is administered by the St. Augustine Historical Society. Guides give house tours, for which there is a charge. The adjacent museum tells the story of St. Augustine and of the people who lived here through the four centuries of the city's history. In **Government House,** at the corner of St. George and King streets, the Historic St. Augustine Preservation Board, an agency of the state of Florida, also runs a museum that tells a more inclusive story of Spanish Florida, including **Fort Mose,** the oldest free black settlement in the United States.

Visiting the Castillo

The Castillo de San Marcos is one of the oldest structures in North America built by Europeans. It is one of the few links on this continent to early modern Europe and a way of warfare that has become obsolete. Park interpreters give frequent programs at the fort telling its history and explaining its construction. They can answer questions you have about the history of the area and about related National Park System sites. You may wish to walk around the Castillo at your own pace; a free park folder available at the entrance station will help you find your way.

A sales outlet to the left of the guard rooms as you enter the Castillo offers books and pamphlets on the history of Florida and Spanish colonization. Some souvenirs and postcards are also available.

Parking is limited at the Castillo and in St. Augustine. Because of the limited parking, therefore, you may wish to take one of the sightseeing tours around the city. Information is available at the Visitor Information Center. For further information about the Castillo de San Marcos and Fort Matanzas, write: Superintendent, Castillo de San Marcos National Monument, 1 Castillo Drive East, St. Augustine, FL 32084.

Beaches

Florida AlA north or south takes you to some of the most beautiful beaches on the east coast. A fee buys a permit from county authorities to drive on county beaches during the summer months. There is also a charge for parking at Anastasia State Recreation Area.

Accommodations

St. Augustine has a variety of accommodations: national chains, locally owned hotels and motels, bed and breakfast inns, and vacation cottages and condominiums for rent by the day, week, or longer.

Other Areas Related to Spanish Florida

Besides Castillo de San Marcos, several other National Park System sites in Florida preserve and interpret aspects of Spanish colonial history. They are located on the map (below) and described on the right hand page.

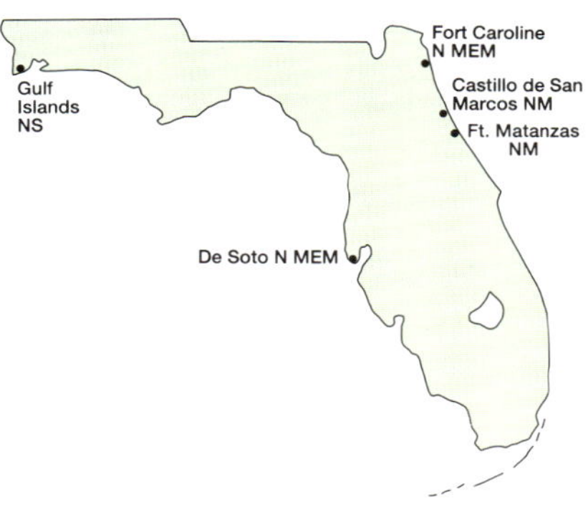

De Soto National Memorial

P.O. Box 16390, Bradenton, FL 34280-5390.

No one knows exactly where Spanish explorer Hernando de Soto landed on Florida's west coast in 1539. This park at the entrance to Tampa Bay memorializes that landing and de Soto's subsequent journeys of exploration throughout the southeastern United States.

Fort Caroline National Memorial

12713 Fort Caroline Road, Jacksonville, FL 32225.

The establishment of a French colony here in 1564 directly challenged the Spaniards, who responded by establishing Saint Augustine the next year. After securing a firm base of operations, the Spaniards led by Pedro Menéndez marched to the French settlement and captured it, ending French interest in the area.

Fort Matanzas National Monument

c/o Castillo de San Marcos National Monument, 1 Castillo Drive, Saint Augustine, FL 32084.

On this site Spanish troops killed French soldiers who were part of the ill-fated attempt to establish a French settlement in Florida. In 1740, after the failed English attack on Saint Augustine, the Spaniards built a masonry fortification—Fort Matanzas—on Rattlesnake Island overlooking Matanzas Inlet to control the inlet permanently.

Gulf Islands National Seashore

1801 Gulf Breeze Parkway, Gulf Breeze, FL 32561.

The ravelin of Fort Barrancas, located on the grounds of the Pensacola Naval Air Station, is another Spanish masonry fortification in Florida besides the Castillo and Fort Matanzas. It is called Battery San Antonio and dates from 1797. It was planned as part of a larger fortification never built by the Spaniards. Fort Barrancas, built by the U.S., dates from the early 19th century.

Besides these parks in Florida there is one in Georgia (not shown on the map) that bears importantly on the story of St. Augustine.

Fort Frederica National Monument

Route 9, Box 286-C, Savannah, GA 31410.

It was at Fort Frederica that James Edward Oglethorpe established a settlement in 1736 only a few days march north of St. Augustine in territory that the Spaniards clearly believed to be their own.

Fort Matanzas National Monument

Fort Caroline National Memorial

National Park Service

National Park Handbooks are published to support
the National Park Service's management programs
and to promote understanding and enjoyment of the
more than 360 National Park System sites that repre-
sent important examples of our country's natural
and cultural inheritance. Each handbook is intended
to be informative reading and a useful guide before,
during, and after a park visit. More than 100 titles
are in print. They are sold at parks and can be pur-
chased by mail from the Superintendent of Docu-
ments, U.S. Government Printing Office, Washington,
DC 20402-9325.

The National Park Service expresses its appreciation
to all those persons who made the preparation and
production of this handbook possible. The text, on
which this handbook is based, was originally written
by Albert Manucy and Luis Arana and appeared as
The Building of the Castillo de San Marcos. The
vault construction, drawbridge, and siege illustrations on pages 33, 34, and 47 are based on artwork
originally developed by Albert Manucy. All photos
and artwork not credited below come from the files
of the Castillo de San Marcos or of the National
Park Service.

Archivo General de Indias, Seville 18, 49
Michael Hampshire 31 (detail), 34
Karen Kasmauski 2-3
Ken Laffal cover, 12, 16, 24, 25, 26 (photographs), 29,
35, 36, 38, 42, 48, 50, 52, 55, 57, 58-59, 60
Library of Congress 4, 10, 26-27 (map), 49
National Geographic Society 14, 15, 22-23
Ken Townsend 30-31, 40-41